# AfterShock

Conflict, Violence and Resolution in Contemporary Art

**AfterShock**

Conflict, Violence and Resolution
in Contemporary Art

Sainsbury Centre for Visual Arts
University of East Anglia
14 July – 2 September 2007
www.scva.ac.uk

University of Hertfordshire Galleries
20 September – 28 October 2007
www.herts.ac.uk/UHgalleries

Curated by Yasmin Canvin
in collaboration with Amanda Geitner, SCVA
and Matthew Shaul, UHG

Sainsbury Centre exhibition design by
George Sexton Associates, Washington DC
Catalogue edited and produced by
Matthew Shaul and Atsuko Kikuchi
Catalogue design by Fraser Muggeridge studio

*AfterShock* is generously supported by Arts Council
England with additional funding from The Charles
Wallace India Trust.

*AfterShock* is presented at the SCVA as part of
Contemporary Art Norwich 07.

The Sainsbury Centre is supported with funds from

The Gatsby Charitable Foundation

Arts & Humanities
Research Council

The Sainsbury Centre is the museum and gallery of

UEA
NORWICH

**Image credits**

The Atlas Group, a project by Walid Raad, *We
Can Make Rain But No One Came To Ask*, courtesy
Anthony Reynolds Gallery, London
T.V. Santhosh, *Another Taxi, Fear, Nation and False
Promises, Peace Protest* and Atul Dodiya, *Page from
a Diary*, photography by Prakash Rao, Mumbai
Alfredo Jaar, *Untitled (Newsweek)* © Alfredo Jaar
Studio
Paul Nash, *We Are Making a New World* © Imperial
War Museum

Every effort has been made to seek permission to
reproduce the images and text in this catalogue whose
copyright does not reside with the Sainsbury Centre
for Visual Arts, and we are grateful to the artists,
individuals and institutions who have assisted us in
this task. Any omissions are entirely unintentional
and the details should be addressed to the Sainsbury
Centre for Visual Arts, University of East Anglia,
Norwich.

cover image:
T.V. Santhosh, *Another Taxi* (detail), 2004
Collection 'The Guild', Mumbai

**Acknowledgements**

We would like to express our gratitude to the artists
participating in *AfterShock* who have made the
exhibition possible. Long conversations have directly
informed the development of the exhibition and
we have also depended on their commitment and
the tireless work of those who assist them. Their
contributions to this catalogue stand alongside their
work as a moving personal testimony to their ability
to face the violence and conflict which is a pervasive
aspect of life in the 21st century.

Arts Council England East has supported *AfterShock*
from the earliest research stages and we are grateful
for its ongoing commitment to the exhibition. The
Charles Wallace India Trust has kindly enabled some
of the Indian artists involved in *AfterShock* to travel
to the UK.

Peter Nagy has been generous with his expertise
throughout the project. Thanks also to Pooja Sood
and Khoj International Artists Association for advice
and introductions that were critical at the very start.
More recently, Anupa Mehta has been on hand to
provide invaluable curatorial liaison in India and
the project has been the richer for her involvement.
We have also regularly depended on Melanie Vial's
swift translations of our correspondence. Atsuko
Kikuchi has worked on the exhibition in her role as
curatorial fellow in cultural diversity and we thank
her for enabling a complex project to come to fruition.
Thanks are also due to the staff at the Sainsbury
Centre and University of Hertfordshire Galleries
who have contributed to the exhibition.

Many of the works included in *AfterShock* have been
very kindly lent by private lenders, to whom we are
greatly indebted. We are most grateful to Gallery
Chemould, The Guild, Merchandani + Steinrucke
and Saffron art, Mumbai, as well as to the Walsh
Gallery, Chicago, and Anthony Reynolds Gallery,
London, for their support of the project and generous
assistance with loans.

Our thanks go to the contributing writers to this
catalogue, who have engaged with the exhibition and
allowed us to approach the work on show from a range
of very different perspectives.

And once again, our thanks to the artists.

*Sainsbury Centre for Visual Arts, UEA Norwich
University of Hertfordshire Galleries*

WORLD ART
COLLECTIONS
EXHIBITIONS     U**H** galleries
SAINSBURY CENTRE
for Visual Arts

# Foreword

University museums and galleries lend themselves particularly well not only to the presentation of art but to the exploration and investigation of its contexts, in ways which some public galleries might find hard to justify. Indeed, many of us believe that we have a mandate to move beyond the surface of the work to stimulate an appreciation of the 'why?' which informs the 'what', particularly when presenting the work of contemporary artists.

The *AfterShock* project is very much about presenting different and highly personal responses to the contexts of conflict. As the texts in this publication demonstrate, these responses can range from the subtly reflective to the unashamedly polemical, with artists' and curatorial voices offering a further set of contexts for engaging with the work on the walls of the gallery. Then there is the yet wider context provided by the Sainsbury Centre for Visual Arts and its outstanding collection of world art, much of which carries, in different ways, its own hidden legacy of conflict. Finally, viewers and readers will inevitably bring to *AfterShock* their own experiences of conflict, whether in their personal lives or as it is delivered to us daily by the world's media.

The overall context for *AfterShock* is, of course, Contemporary Art Norwich 07. Inaugurated in 2005, Contemporary Art Norwich offers both 'locals' and visitors not only new opportunities for collective working but a wonderfully rich mix of art, artists and curatorial approaches. For this the thanks must go to Arts Council England, and particularly to the staff in the eastern region, whose energy and persistence have made this second Contemporary Art Norwich 07 such a diverse and enriching experience. We at the Sainsbury Centre would also like to acknowledge the commitment of *AfterShock's* guest curator, Yasmin Canvin, and this publication's commissioning editor, Matthew Shaul, in whose gallery at the University of Hertfordshire a version of the exhibition will be shown later this year.

*Nichola Johnson*
*Director, Sainsbury Centre for Visual Arts*
*May 2007*

# Far from the Epicentre

This exhibition project began in 2003 with a trip to India organised by Arts Council England for some 20 regionally based UK curators. We travelled to Delhi, Jaipur and Mumbai to look at contemporary art and craft practice. A clear memory from that first shock of vivid days was our meeting with Gigi Scaria and the Khoj International Artists Association in New Delhi. A few days later we saw Gigi, and many of the other artists we met at Khoj, at an exhibition to celebrate 40 years of the commercial Gallery Chemould at the National Gallery of Modern Art, Mumbai. That night India's close-knit contemporary art community was out in force. The opening event was our first opportunity to see a large body of current work. We began to understand that, though artists were much in demand for international projects and exhibitions, large-scale venues for showing exhibitions in India were few. The art market was strong and new work was swiftly sold, primarily to private collectors. As a result, there was little work to be seen in artists' studios. We had been dependent on seeing work in reproduction in catalogues; that night we were impressed by the strength of the work on show.

Eighteen months later, four of the curators on that original visit (Yasmin Canvin, Matthew Shaul, Barbara Taylor and I) returned to take a more focused look at contemporary Indian art. Yasmin Canvin, who organised this Arts Council funded trip, had recently been appointed lead curatorial fellow in cultural diversity for the Arts Council. This time our attention was directed toward a number of artists whose work had struck us in 2003, but the desired outcome of our research was still unclear. From the outset, Yasmin was interested in depictions of violence or conflict in its broadest terms – social, political, communal, international, domestic. What we found compelling was the filtered, indirect approach to issues of violence – a use of media images distorted, repainted or reversed, or a film about two young boys living on the streets which gently drew you towards an understanding of one particular strategy for survival amid crushing urban poverty. Much of the work we saw was also very beautiful, allowing us to stay with it long enough to consider the circumstances it addressed.

Through conversations with the artists we met, it became clear that they were keen to avoid being 'festivalised'. There were a number of Indian shows in progress in which work was admired for its distinctive 'Indian-ness'. What we heard from artists was a desire to be shown abroad and at home, in context with other artists working internationally, in exhibitions in which the issues addressed by their work were of primary importance.

Two curators working in India were valuable sounding boards during our early research. Pooja Sood, director of Khoj in New Delhi, is immensely well networked, generous with her time, a passionate supporter of many artists and a perceptive and incisive critic of others. Anupa Mehta (based in Mumbai and more recently in Ahmadabad) challenged us, probing our choices and impressions, daring us not to allow our fascination with all things Indian to lead to our seduction by work that was exotic and enticing, but ultimately conceptually weak. They encouraged us to remain receptive to elements and visual strategies that were specifically Indian, while bringing our own critical standards to bear.

This second trip enabled us to identify a core group of artists with whom we wanted to work – Atul Dodiya, Shilpa Gupta, Jitish Kallat, T.V. Santhosh and Gigi Scaria – and it was from their work the exhibition developed. Yasmin identified other UK-based and international artists and discussed their work with Matthew and me. Each inclusion was considered between us and so the show grew, with each body of work seen in relationship to the others. What bound the selection was a reflection on violence and conflict, directly or indirectly experienced, represented at some remove. Away from the epicentre of the event, the works all examine the aftermath, the outward reverberation of influence or effect. Each work represented an attempt to come to terms with violent events or proposed a way of understanding the onslaught of distressing images that we face or ignore each day.

What emerged from the work was an emphasis on a particular approach to violent subjects. We did not set out to represent within the exhibition all the sites of international conflict in the last decade, nor were we determined to exclusively represent those that have been particularly high-profile. It was not our intention that we necessarily learn anything about the political and social contexts to which they refer from the art works. Instead, we were attracted to work that told us as much about how we respond, try and sometimes fail to understand images of conflict and violence in our own environment. Many of these works draw our attention back to what it feels like to sit in front of our televisions, computers and newspapers trying to make sense of mass and individual violence. Do we understand these images at all? As we become desensitised to them do we lose something of ourselves? As events become no longer newsworthy, the works in *AfterShock* remind us of the lasting impact of violence and the need for memory and memorial. At times we asked ourselves what relevance the work in the exhibition has to us in the peaceful region of East Anglia – but we live alongside groups who have fled violence and in communities in which issues of race, domestic violence and gun crime are an increasing concern. We need to understand them.

*Amanda Geitner*
*Head of Collections and Exhibitions*
*Sainsbury Centre for Visual Arts*

Roger Fenton, *The Valley of the Shadow of Death*, 1855
Colour film copy transparency printed on salted paper
28 × 36 cm

# Presence through Absence and the Art of Slowing Down

In the 21st century socially or politically driven conflict and violence has become an omnipresent backdrop to our lives. There are over 40 wars being fought in the world today, including the ubiquitous 'war on terror', and daily we hear of domestic abuse, gang violence, child abuse, and knife and gun crime through the press and media. There are enormous challenges, however, associated with an artistic engagement with these issues. Roland Barthes, for example, argued that shocking photographs 'limit the sight by force, stop language and defeat imagination'. While Susan Sontag wrote 'Harrowing photographs... are not much help if the task is to understand.' She does, however, acknowledge the power of storytelling, adding, 'Narratives can make us understand.'[1]

In contrast to other artists dealing with similar themes, such as Jake and Dinos Chapman, whose sculptures of mutilated bodies have a shocking, visceral impact, or Langland's and Bell's emotionless virtual tour of Bin Laden's hideaway in Afghanistan, the artists in *AfterShock* build narratives and subtly engage the viewer in their thought processes. This approach has a long history in western contemporary art. Photographer Roger Fenton (1819–69) is considered to be one of the pioneers of war photography, yet when 'embedded' with British troops in the Crimea in the mid-1850s, he took no images of the war itself. There were many reasons for this; his bulky equipment slowed him down and restricted his practice, and there were political and commercial concerns to consider as he was enjoying the support of the British government and had a publisher for the work. Yet his most famous image[2] (opposite) tells a harrowing story of war through the emptiness of a desolate landscape depicting only the aftermath of fighting. The British soldiers had named the site the 'Valley of Death' due to the continuous shelling; the used cannonballs were appropriate metaphors for the dead. The painter Paul Nash (1889–1946) was an official war artist during both world wars and created atmospheric paintings using a muted colour palette to portray the hollow aftermath of war. In one image, a soldier's helmet remains on the ground in memoriam of its owner. In another work (overleaf), a forest of dark, broken trees and a brooding, red sky testify to recent violence. Later, back in Britain, as his close family members died and his physical and mental health deteriorated, he continued to paint trees, in the form of dead elms or pale skeletal shadows, to represent corpses, expressing the death of men through nature.

In a similar way, the artists in *AfterShock* have developed their own strategies to depict violence and suffering without shocking: they show us alternative histories, create dialogues between real and imagined narratives, recontextualise images, use subtle, seductive or fragmented images and sometimes even employ humour. While the artists focus on the moments before and after violence has occurred, or on the effects of conflict, they do not take sides. Instead, through video,

photography and reworked images, these artists articulate the voice of the individual, producing poignant, personal responses to the conflict and violence they have either directly or indirectly experienced. The artists' different experiences are equally valid, whether they are responding to violence within their own community, or to the global effects of conflict elsewhere. Violence and conflict is not restricted to the battlefield: since the first world war approximately three quarters of all war deaths have been civilians and entire cities have become military or terrorist targets.

**Alfredo Jaar** has stated that, 'our society is blind; we have lost our ability to be affected by imagery'[3]. In order to counteract this tendency he constructs photo, text and light installations, which encourage viewers to use their imagination. When Jaar first returned from Rwanda in 1994, he was so severely affected by what he had seen that he was unable to use the images he had taken. Instead, his first work featured the country's name in huge light-boxes. For a subsequent work titled *Real Pictures*, he hid the photographs in archival boxes, only the description on the outside indicated the horrors he had witnessed. These were exhibited as tombstone-like memorials. In a later piece, *Untitled (Newsweek)*, he showed 17 front covers of the journal alongside text describing what had been happening in Rwanda that week and the cumulative total of deaths during the genocide from 6 April to 1 August 1994. The work powerfully portrays the lack of action taken by the rest of the world as Rwandans massacred each other. Through looking and reading, the viewer is physically slowed down so that each image and line of text receives their full attention.

By comparison, Bill Viola, discussing his film work, has spoken about how the concept of time – an abstract idea – was made tangible through the invention of clocks and thereby the construction of a 'physical unit' of time. Although segments of time are constant throughout the day, they vary in length according to our perception of them. Viola refers to the effects achieved by slowing down a film; this not only reveals otherwise invisible gestures that go unnoticed because of their speed in 'normal time' but also shows how what appears to be a momentary single emotion can contain infinite variations.

*A Season Outside*, **Amar Kanwar's** personal and poignant meditation on violence and non-violence, seems to step outside of time, bringing the past and present together. The film depicts the absurd movements of the Pakistani and Indian border control guards as they high-step to the gate at the Wagah-Atari border in the Punjab, while groups of Muslims and Hindus on either side look on. At one point, time seems to slow down, as the viewer becomes aware of every detail of the guards' uniforms. The painted white border line takes on immense significance through the guards' actions, the weight of history – as it recalls the violence between the two nations during partition (in 1947) – and the constant threat of violence continuing until today. The film concludes with grainy scenes of Mahatma Gandhi and of Kanwar's own contemplation of non-violence.

**Atul Dodiya's** text paintings are from a series based on Gandhi's statement that he was 'only an artist of non-violence and desired to develop the art of non-violence in the realm of resistance.'[4] Gandhi's motivation was an aesthetic one: that of restoring balance, harmony and therefore beauty to a society that had been thrown into turmoil by violence. It is a challenge for an artist to portray such an iconic figure, one whose whole life was lived in the public realm and in the media, to such an extent that certain well-known images have supplanted actual memories of those events. Dodiya used the qualities of watercolour to create a new portrait of Gandhi, focusing our attention on different aspects of otherwise familiar scenes, or, in the cases of *Page from a Diary* and *Sale of Khadi*, he used real and imaginary documents from Gandhi's life as metaphors of history. These paintings bypass iconography and allow the viewer to imagine what Gandhi was like and what momentous events could be scrawled in a personal diary. In *The Route to Dandi*, the viewer is left to visualise their own account of the Salt March protest of 1930.[5]

Jitish Kallat and T.V. Santhosh are interested in how the media shapes and constructs our understanding of current events and they examine the workings of the media through its own imagery. **Jitish Kallat** is also interested in the specific ways violence is depicted and references popular culture. In the *The Lie of the Land* paintings he reworks images familiar to those living in India; the well-planned politician's photo opportunity, the riots and the injured being stretchered away. Viewers have to ascertain 'the lie of the land' for themselves, piecing the narrative together from 'disturbed found images' which have been blown with a vacuum cleaner while the paint is still wet and the work 'almost begins to bleed' as Kallat 're-enacts the stance of a perpetrator-gunman during the act of painting'. The resulting images are 'blown, splattered and interrupted by red masses and text'[6]. Although this work is based specifically in the Indian context, Kallat's paintings reference universal political and social structures and invite the viewer to recognise their own local situations within them.

In his diptychs, **T.V. Santhosh** paints positive and negative images drawn from press photographs to indicate that the 'truth' is not represented by the images in the media, or in any other image, but somewhere in between. In *Another Taxi*, for example, the dead body is only visible on one half of the work; on the other it forms part of the background. Santhosh says, 'As certain elements get deleted and become unrecognisable, they reveal an event's hidden implications. My works deal with devised glimpses of much larger, unresolved stories of immediate happenings'.[7] Another work, *Your Terrorist Our Freedom Fighter*, refers to the way the same image and news story is read and understood differently when viewed from opposing sides of the same conflict, and how images and facts are manipulated or concealed in an attempt to portray a single version of the 'truth'. The result is that it is difficult to find agreement and resolutions remain elusive.

François Bucher, Gigi Scaria and Simon Norfolk present alternative narratives to those provided by the media. Video footage shot during the attacks on 11 September 2001 was immediately broadcast around the world and the whole event seemed unreal to many. During the aftermath we heard about the bravery of the rescuers and how the city, and by inference the American people, picked itself up and carried on. During this time, **François Bucher** took a video camera onto the streets of New York. The resulting work; *White Balance (to think is to forget differences)* is a video montage of shots of Lower Manhattan before and after the attack; maps, web pages, press clips, texts by the artist, statistics, immigration identikits, scenes from Hollywood films and passages of digital scrambling. Bucher shows us another side to those events – the mixed emotions, the confusion, the moneymaking schemes – demonstrating that people are not just heroes or cowards, victims or terrorists.

2007 is the 60th anniversary of the partition of India, a political decision that brought great violence and trauma to the Indian subcontinent. Gandhi consistently stated that violence could not solve problems or alleviate suffering. He was, however, implicated in the failure to find a peaceful solution for the future of India and therefore many have since rejected his ideas. **Gigi Scaria's** *Raise your hands those who have touched him* attempts to re-examine the teachings of Gandhi through those who knew him and investigate what role they might play in a world 'transformed through corporate logic and capitalism', full of 'culturally and religiously aggressive communities'[8]. Scaria films 'from inside' and as a result awards great dignity to the ordinary people he portrays in his work and to their memories. This 'leads to further recognitions'[9] which grant the viewer an understanding of an otherwise foreign situation, as we come to appreciate the significance of Gandhi's death, indicated by the gradual revealing of his wound in the video.

Although photographs only show fragments of a whole scene, most photographers focus the viewer's eyes inwards. In **Simon Norfolk's** work the viewer is also encouraged to look beyond the page, to consider the context of the photographs, in terms of time and place: what occurred before and after, in the next building or on the next street. Although the actual places may seem familiar to us through the immediacy of 24-hour global news coverage, Norfolk's images provide us with a more considered insight. Through focusing attention on the detailed impact of war – the loss of a cinema, a library, or other architecturally monumental buildings – Norfolk shows war's destruction of historic cultures and portrays other hidden aspects, such as the creation of a technological culture of surveillance. The series *Ascension Island: The Panopticon*[10] highlights one of the most interesting yet least discussed developments of warfare, that of electronic weaponry. Norfolk's photographs transform the still, lifeless antennae into sentinel beings; as we look at them they seem to be looking back at us. Even the island's landscape betrays its use as a weapon of war.

*Kidnapped: homage to Karachi*, a video work by **Alia Hasan-Khan** transports the viewer to another place of fear and

Paul Nash, *We Are Making a New World*, 1918
Oil on canvas
71 × 91 cm
Imperial War Museum, London

constant surveillance: that of a kidnap victim. It shows the actual point of view of the victim as they lie on the back seat of a car as it travels from the leafy suburbs into the violence-torn city. The voices of the two kidnappers are heard as they discuss comparatively banal matters – what to buy for lunch, the price of food in the local market. The fictional narrative enables the viewer to contemplate the possible reaction of an individual in these circumstances. We wonder whether the victim can understand the kidnappers' language, is it a familiar or an unfamiliar journey? Kidnapping has become a common occurrence in Karachi, the largest city in Pakistan, as in many other major cities around the world where there is a huge disparity in wealth. However, the work could equally relate to kidnapping used as a weapon of war, as a tool of terrorists or governments.

Dave Lewis and Walid Raad create narratives, through a combination of fact and fiction, which challenge accepted histories and dismantle the supposed autonomy of art. **Dave Lewis's** photographic series, *Chapter Six – Racism*, comments on the impact of the enquiry into the death of Stephen Lawrence in London in 1993 on his own black community and, by implication, on the wider community in general. The enquiry was commissioned by the Home Office to establish the causes behind the failure to convict anyone for the murder of Stephen Lawrence. Lewis uses brief sections of the Report as subtexts to the activities of a fictional black man going about his everyday life. Sometimes the images seem to corroborate the text; at other times they challenge its meaning. The work suggests that we need to question the power of images and what is widely accepted as truth and fact.

**Walid Raad** established The Atlas Group in 1999 as an imaginary foundation to research and document the recent history of Lebanon, including the late 20th-century civil war, kidnappings and car bombs, while simultaneously examining the manner in which history is written and compiled. The Atlas Group archive contains authored, found, and newly produced files by imaginary historians such as Dr Fadl Fakhouri, as well as actual press archives. Raad discusses the notion of historical records: 'Traditional history tends to concentrate on what really happened, as if it's out there in the world, and it tends to be the history of conscious events. Most people's experience of these events… is predominantly unconscious and concentrates on facts, objects, experiences, and feelings that leave traces and should be collected.'[11] Those traces, in essence, are The Atlas Group's archive. One of them, the video *We Can Make Rain But No One Came To Ask*, 'documents' a collaboration between Yussef Bitar, the Lebanese state's leading ammunitions expert and chief investigator of all car bomb detonations, and Georges Semerdjian, a respected photojournalist, during a detonation in Beirut in 1986.

Fernando Traverso, David Farrell and Juan Manuel Echavarría claim difficult histories of individuals, that few others have dared to investigate, through their works, which are extraordinary explorations of how people and ideas can be powerfully present though physically absent. **Fernando Traverso's** work *350, Intervención urbana* is an intervention

in the streets where he lived. He worked in the resistance during the military dictatorship (1976–83) in Argentina until he was forced to go into exile. During that time 29 of his friends disappeared; in total, 350 citizens of Rosario were 'disappeared' during the 'Dirty War'.[12] An abandoned bicycle was often the first sign that someone had been kidnapped or 'disappeared' since bicycles were the most common form of transport for members of the resistance. Traverso secretly spray-painted 350 images of bicycles throughout the city and photographed each one. These bicycles became memorials for the disappeared and metaphors of absence. Traverso refers to the Tao: 'it's not only the contour, but the emptiness too that allows reality to attain an ultimate meaning.'[13]

**David Farrell** wanted to make work that responded to the complexities surrounding 'The Troubles' in Northern Ireland, but as a 'southerner' he felt unable to until 1999, when he was staying at Monaghan near the border and the searches for 'the disappeared' began. The first of these burial sites was at Colgagh, and it quickly became apparent that all the sites of 'the disappeared' were situated in the Republic of Ireland. Farrell was drawn to the searches by the 'double wrong': the actual murder followed by the withholding of the body from the grieving relatives. Farrell comments on the 'overwhelming sense of presence/absence and violence he felt as he observed the violated landscape where the bodies of two young men had been found'.[14] He revisits and photographs these sites every year, noting the subtle changes to the landscape.

**Juan Manuel Echavarría** responds through his work to the normality of violence in his community as a result of the Colombian drug wars. Without preconceived ideas about how he was going to portray the victims he visited the site where bodies were being washed up[15] and spoke to those living nearby. They told him about people who had witnessed terrible massacres and described their experiences through the region's narrative tradition, through song. In turn, through Echavarría's work they are reaching out to audiences all over the world. The absence of violent imagery portrays the effects of violence more strikingly than any horror scene could. Alfredo Jaar spoke about this when he reflected on his visit to Rwanda: 'I have always been concerned with the disjunction between experience and what can be recorded photographically. In the case of Rwanda, the disjunction was enormous and the tragedy unrepresentable. This is why it was so important for me to speak with people, to record their words, their ideas, their feelings. I discovered that the truth of the tragedy was in the feelings, words, and ideas of those people, and not in the pictures.'[16] It is difficult to see the faces of those who have survived terrible massacres and listen to their stories. Yet it can be cathartic for those who have also suffered great pain.

Ian Charlesworth's and Shilpa Gupta's work examines how the ubiquitous imagery derived from wars and conflict can become part of everyday life. **Ian Charlesworth** mimics the graffiti thoughtlessly left behind by individuals on the walls of toilets and other public places in Northern Ireland, which affiliate the protagonist to the UVF (Ulster Volunteer Force). The UVF is a loyalist paramilitary organisation, with a violent history, yet these marks have become almost meaningless. Charlesworth uses cigarette lighters – the same technique used by the graffitists – to produce seductive, abstracted forms of the letters on the ceiling of the gallery, creating a deceptively beautiful environment. Taking the symbols out of their usual context causes the viewer to question their meaning and usage.

**Shilpa Gupta** draws attention to common yet significant local issues that have a global impact. Her previous projects have addressed religion, terrorism and the value of human life. In *Untitled* (2004) the seven life-sized projected figures are dressed in camouflage, which has become increasingly fashionable in India since 'the war on terror' campaign. The viewer can manipulate the figures by selecting and directing the actions of the 'leader' and the actions are then copied by the other figures. These actions are 'subtitled': some of the phrases are innocent exercise cues, while others challenge free speech, the free market, and war and terrorism. An uneasy sense of tragic comedy pervades the work. As we interact with it we are forced to consider our own attitudes towards the violence surrounding us and carried out on our behalf. How did war become a fashion statement or a game? And who is controlling whom?

The second work by **Jitish Kallat**, *Cenotaph (A Deed of Transfer)* examines another form of social violence. Kallat took the photographs after he witnessed the demolition of a squatter settlement on the streets of Mumbai and he 'decided to work through the images such that every element in the photograph and every residue of aggression gets activated'. Later he observed that 'the supporting wall against which these houses were built had been re-absorbed as a city wall and slowly film posters and advertising bills were being pasted on them.'[17] The lenticular prints take on a three-dimensionality as the viewer moves around them, almost placing the viewer in the abandoned buildings.

Like many of the artists in *AfterShock*, Kallat personalises and memorialises events that would otherwise simply become historical fact and then be forgotten by the majority. Television and newspaper journalists use personal 'human interest' angles to draw our attention to significant local and international news, yet this is often done in a superficial way. Gandhi wrote: 'In the very first month of *Indian Opinion* [a journal he founded in 1904], I realised that the sole aim of journalism should be service. The newspaper press is a great power, but just as an unchained torrent of water submerges whole countrysides and devastates crops, even so an uncontrolled pen serves but to destroy. If the control is from without, it proves more poisonous than want of control. It can be profitable only when exercised from within. If this line of reasoning is correct, how many of the journals in the world would stand the test? But who would stop those that are useless? And who should be the judge? The useful and the useless must, like good and evil generally, go on together and man must make his choice.'[18] Gandhi would doubtless feel the same way about all forms of mass media today. Sociologist Herbert J. Gans wrote the following with regard to television: '...the primary purpose of the news derives from the journalists' functions as constructors of nation and society, and as managers of the symbolic arena'.[19] The news channels may feign objectivity, but they do not wield their power in an open or neutral way. Britain has recently marked the 25 anniversary of the Falklands war, yet during the war itself only two photojournalists were granted access and no direct television transmission was permitted. The Gulf War was famous for its night images of a highly technological war – a war fought at a distance through reconnaissance and targeted 'precision' bombings – but not of the casualties left in their wake.

David Levi Strauss writes that 'Artists cannot compete with the Pandaemonium on its own terms; they are outgunned and vastly undercapitalised. The only way to effectively subvert it is to change the rules of engagement, to engage the audience differently.'[20] The artists in *AfterShock* achieve this by employing different strategies; some follow on from the work of Magnum photographer Robert Capa (1913–54) and focus on the impact of violence on the individual, rather than the vast numbers affected by conflict. Other artists encourage the viewer to pause and reflect on the images before them, to question and create their own meanings. In this sense, these art works also exist as a form of memento mori, as objects that can be used for contemplation. Susan Sontag makes the point that 'to remember is, more and more, not to recall a story but to be able to call up a picture.'[21] The images act as memorials; as the individuals involved pass away, or the locations depicted become overgrown or are absorbed by urban development, while Echavarría's work memorialises the survivors through narratives, through their unforgettable songs.

In some instances, the same media image is shown again and again until it replaces the actual memory of the event. As one writer commented 'Sept. 11 was the most widely transmitted visual event in history, represented, however, by just a few photographic images whose ubiquity on front pages was due to the concentration of power in the hands of "a reduced number of broadcasters." ... A century and a half after the Crimean photographs (of Roger Fenton), second-by-second images of the planes going into the towers, of the fireballs and the plumes of smoke and of the dust-white office workers fleeing, terrified and stunned, became inseparable from the event itself for people around the globe. No longer were pictures from the battlefront as unfamiliar and foreign as the places where they were shot; they now functioned as a means of transference. More than recording the experience, they became it'.[22] *AfterShock* investigates how images are used in contemporary culture and offers alternative spaces to encourage us to think about what we are being shown and what we engage with when we play video games, when we decide what to wear, when we watch the news, read the newspapers or other historical accounts.

In many ways, the resolution referred to in the subtitle of this exhibition alludes to the actions of the viewer as they contemplate their personal circumstances, as well as the artists' resolution of the difficulties faced when creating work that tackles such complex and emotive issues. Susan Sontag argues that 'People don't become inured to what they are shown...

because of the quantity of images dumped on them. It is passivity that dulls feeling.'[23] These artists are not passive to the violence and conflict around them and, as a result, their work poses pertinent questions to the viewer; how might they react if it was happening in their own back yard? Although some of the work responds to violence and conflict in faraway places, the issues raised also have a profound local resonance: refugees to Britain are often fleeing violent circumstances,[24] displacement is present in London as homes, businesses and ancient allotments are bulldozed to make way for the 2012 Olympics, British soldiers are currently involved in ongoing conflicts in Iraq and Afghanistan, journalists, business people and children are kidnapped while abroad, many British Asians carry the scars of the partition, the bombings in London on 7 July 2005 have impacted on the whole community and despite recent historical events, tensions from the Troubles in Northern Ireland have not yet disappeared. *AfterShock* demonstrates that although each experience of conflict or violence is unique, it is possible to find empathy with the suffering of others, and that there can be a powerful link between life and art when we create the reality within our imagination and make our own connections.

*Yasmin Canvin*
*Freelance Curator and Writer*

This exhibition was developed while Canvin was employed as the lead curatorial fellow – Cultural Diversity, Arts Council England East

1. Susan Sontag, *Regarding the Pain of Others*, Penguin Books, England, 2004, p. 80.
2. This is one of only two photographs taken at the same site. In the other image, there are no cannonballs on the roadway itself. Two reasons have been suggested to explain this; either Fenton placed them there for effect, or they were removed for use by the army.
3. Alfredo Jaar, artist's statement.
4. Catalogue for Atul Dodiya's exhibition *An artist of non-violence*, Gallery Chemould, India, 1999, preface.
5. The 200-mile walk was a protest against the British taxation of salt.
6. Jitish Kallat, artist's statement, e-mail conversation.
7. T.V. Santhosh, artist's statement.
8. Gigi Scaria, artist's statement, e-mail conversation.
9. David Levi Strauss, 'Between the Eyes; Essays on Photography and Politics', *Aperture*, New York, 2003, p. 48, writing about Sebastao Salgado's work: 'Looking, one realizes how different they are from other photographs… Whereas those other images end at pity or compassion, Salgado's images begin at compassion and lead from there to further recognitions. One of the first of these further recognitions is that starvation does not obliterate human dignity.'
10. A chapter from *Et in Arcadia ego*, a project through which Simon Norfolk attempts 'to understand how war and the need to fight war, has formed our world: how so many of the spaces we occupy; the technologies we use and the ways we understand ourselves, are created by military conflict'.
11. Walid Raad, artist's statement.
12. In Spanish: *Guerra Sucia*; the name given to the state-sponsored illegal arrest, torture, killing or forced disappearance of thousands of citizens in Argentina, mostly carried out by Jorge Rafael Videla's military government.
13. Fernando Traverso, artist's statement.
14. David Farrell, artist's statement, e-mail conversation.
15. The title of the work, *Bocas de Ceniza/Mouths of Ash*, relates to the name of the estuary of the Magdalena River where the corpses appeared.
16. Alfredo Jaar, quoted by David Levi Strauss, ibid., p. 92.
17. Jitish Kallat, artist's statement, e-mail conversation.
18. Mahatma Gandhi, *An autobiography or the story of my experiments with Truth*, Navajivan Publishing House, 1920–29, p. 349.
19. Herbert J. Gans, *Deciding What's News: A study of CBS Evening News, NBC Nightly News, Newsweek and Time*, New York, Pantheon, 1979.
20. David Levi Strauss, ibid., p. 164.
21. Susan Sontag, ibid., p. 80.
22. Michael Kimmelman, The International Herald Tribune, 23 March 2007.
23. Susan Sontag, ibid., p. 91.
24. Norwich has been designated as the UK's first City of Refuge for persecuted and threatened writers.

# The Atlas Group /
# Walid Raad

The Atlas Group is a project established by
Walid Raad in 1999 to research and document the
contemporary history of war in his native Lebanon.
The project's public forms include mixed-media
installations, single channel screenings, visual and
literary essays, and lectures/performances.

Walid Raad was born in 1967 and grew up in
Lebanon. He is a media artist and an assistant
professor of art at Cooper Union (New York, USA)
where he now lives and works.

He is also a member of the Arab Image Foundation,
started in 1996 to promote historical research of
the visual culture of the Arab world, and to promote
experimental video production in the region.

His work has been shown at Documenta; The
Kunstern Festival des Arts, Brussels; The Vienna
Festival; The Whitney Biennial, New York; The
Alyoul Festival, Beirut; and numerous other festivals
and major public museums and galleries across
Europe, the Middle East and North America. He
has recently been awarded the Deutsche Börse
Photography Prize 2007.

The Atlas Group is a project founded by Walid Raad in Beirut in 1999 to research and document the 'history of Lebanon of the past 50 years with particular emphasis on the history of Lebanon since 1975'. The group retrieves, preserves, analyses, and produces audiovisual, photographic, literary and other documents. These are organised into a specially created archive located in Beirut and New York. The dating, number, origin and form of the documents change depending on the type of presentation or performance. Far from arbitrary, this practice seeks to deconstruct the obligatory forms of the authentic. The dividing line between fact and fiction becomes blurred... This enables the process of historical reinterpretation in the first place, whereby other 'truths' come to light. How does one narrate/research history?... Authentic truth is only a construct and is defined anew from each specific present.

The work shown in *AfterShock* imagines a collaboration between Yussef Bitar, the Lebanese state's leading ammunitions expert and chief investigator of all car bomb detonations, and Georges Semerdjian, a respected photo-journalist and videographer, who, until his violent death in 1990 tirelessly chronicled the Lebanese wars of the past three decades. The videotape focuses on diagrams, notes, videotapes and photographs produced by Bitar and Semerdjian about a detonation in the Furn Ech Chubak neighbourhood of Beirut on 21 January 1986.

Raad may be understood as a pivotal protagonist of an artistic discourse that manoeuvres its way between the conceptions of Western and (Middle) Eastern views of the world, society, and art, and in the process constantly undermines the respective predominant patterns of perception and orders of knowledge. Raad focuses on questions which can be undoubtedly characterised as existential. They are questions about subjective impressions and personal experience, about how individuals remember and fabricate 'history'. In The Atlas Group project and its archive these questions are posed in the form of – fictive and mostly 'private' – documents of everyday life in Lebanon, particularly in the years of the Lebanese civil wars. 'Official' historiography fixes these wars to a period between 1975 and 1990–91. But the work of Walid Raad and The Atlas Group unerringly persists in tracing the continuing effect these war experiences exert right up to the present and the fragility of personal recollection. Highlighting the shortcomings of a historical discourse obsessed with facts, in their sheer resilience against reductive representations, these works point beyond the momentary.

*The Atlas Group (1989–2004) A Project by Walid Raad, exhibition catalogue, 2006, Verlag der Buchhandlung Walter König, Köln, p. 39, 41, 42, 120.*

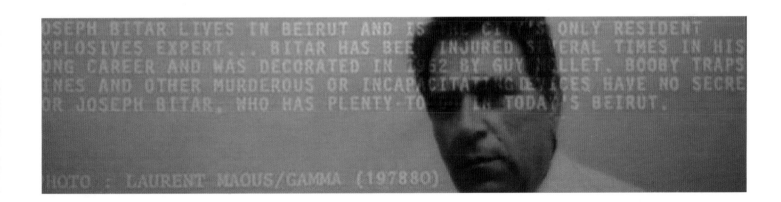

**We Can Make Rain But No One Came To Ask** 2005
Video still
Courtesy Anthony Reynolds Gallery, London

**We Can Make Rain But No One Came To Ask**  2005
Video stills
Courtesy Anthony Reynolds Gallery, London

# François Bucher

François Bucher was born in Cali, Colombia in 1972.
He studied art and literature at the Universidad de los
Andes, Bogotá, Colombia, and went on to complete
a master of fine arts in film at the School of the Art
Institute of Chicago in 1999, where he was awarded
a fellowship. In the following year, he participated in
The Whitney Museum Independent Study Program,
New York. Since 2005, he has been a visiting
professor at Umeå University, Academy of Fine Arts,
Umeå, Sweden.

Bucher's work has been exhibited internationally
in solo and group exhibitions and in film festivals.
His work *White Balance* has won international film
festival awards including the Werkleitz Award,
Transmediale Festival, Berlin, 2004; First Prize,
Premio a la Videocreation en Iberoamerica, MUSAC,
Casa de America, Madrid, 2004; Director's Citation,
Black Maria Film Festival, 2004; First Prize, Video
EX International Experimental Film and Video
Festival, Zurich, 2003; and Prize of the Jury,
Videolisboa, Lisboa, 2003. He is also the co-editor
of *Valdez Magazine*, Bogotá, and has published
a number of essays.

Bucher lives and works in Berlin.

I like the notion that all images are sleeping in the expectation of the moment of their awakening. This is my feeling about the task many of us who are working with the images of the media have taken on. I understand the politics of pieces such as *White Balance (to think is to forget differences)* much more in the dimension of the 'how' than in the dimension of the 'why'. By this I mean that my most essential political quest is, firstly, a practice that comes up with an unitary compact universal thesis and then finds the images that will illustrate it, in order to convert the spectator to a new higher truth. I find myself at a radical distance from a practice that is self-assured in that fashion. When speaking about *White Balance (to think is to forget differences)* I have always brought about a quote from Osip Mandelstam: 'where there is [an] amenability to paraphrase, where the sheets have not been rumpled, there poetry, so to speak, has not spent the night.' The rumpled sheets are my politics. In an investigation from *inside* the image (where, Jean-Luc Godard has always emphasized, the *political* position lies – in opposition the Hollywood script), something powerful takes place when the artist shepherds the image as a force that is beyond him, a constellation of forces that exceed him, when he realises up front that an image resides only temporarily with him, that it has a life and a history of its own. I am not referring to an arbitrary operation, because it all comes from a pointed, initially imageless, intuition that needs the time-image to *come to light*. Continuing with another Deleuzian notion I am very attuned to the notion that ideas are suspended within a medium, one that grows out of (pre-existing) film, not an idea that will later be translated to film. With *White Balance (to think is to forget differences)*, for example, I started out with the idea of making a conjugation of the technical instructions from a camera manual and 'racial politics' as an effort to give the matter the complexity that it deserves and to reach the 'layers of unspeakability' that it truly implies. Privilege and race are always speaking to us (we are spoken to by them), not the other way around.

*François Bucher*

**White Balance (to think is to forget differences)**  2002
Video stills

# Ian Charlesworth

Ian Charlesworth was born in 1970 and currently lives and works in Belfast. He gained a BA (Hons) fine art in 1992 from De Montfort University, Leicester and received his master of fine art from the University of Ulster in 1998. In 2005–06, he was an Arts Council of Northern Ireland Fellow at the British School in Rome.

His work explores the basis of representation in drawing and photography and has been exhibited nationally and internationally.

Selected solo and group exhibitions include *Dogs Have No Religion*, Czech Musuem of Fine Arts, Prague, 2006; *Crossing*, Lipoli and Lopez Gallery, Rome 2006; *Overlap 3*, The British School at Rome, 2006; *The Nature of Things*, Venice Biennale, Northern Ireland Exhibition, 2005; *The Belfast Way*, Herzilya Museum of Contemporary Art, Tel Aviv, 2005; and Jerwood Drawing Prize exhibitions 2003 and 2004.

The work of Ian Charlesworth can best be introduced through its two distinct strands. The first is work consisting of pictorial surfaces marked by a continuous series of black horizontal lines. These lines are made from drawing a lighted candle or burning matches across the surface, whether it be a primed wooden board or the ceiling of a particular gallery space. These can be called the *line* works.

This mark-making touches on the heroic mode all too often ascribed to key figures in the canon of art. Think of the figure of Charlton Heston as Michelangelo (*The Agony and the Ecstasy*) lying beneath the ceiling of the Sistine Chapel, or, of Namuth's film work creating the 'heroic' Pollock amidst the act of creation. Now think of Charlesworth, lying beneath his work, candle in hand, creating a pictorial surface from gestural action. To give the resultant work titles such as *I Do, None, None* – an obvious play on The Crystal's pop classic (*I do run, run*) – is to rob any action from heroic intent. Action is rendered harrowingly glib. All that remains in the wake of the trace is the idea of the subject forever in the process of its making.

The second strand is work developing this mark-making in relation to graffiti found in charged urban spaces around Northern Ireland. The UVF scrawl – a direct reference to the proscribed loyalist paramilitary group in Northern Ireland – is often found burned onto the ceilings of pub toilet cubicles from cheap cigarette lighters. Charlesworth reproduces the technique, charring gesso boards before sealing them with an acrylic resin. One piece is limited to a repeated chain of UVF marks while others continue to build one scrawl upon the previous. The result is a perpetual layering of text upon text to the point where the initial act of mimesis threatens to vanish beyond recall.

By drawing the UVF scrawl into the exhibition space, a tension is set up between its toilet-wall origins and its sanitised destination. It is not simply the mark that is called into question but the confines in which it appears *as art*.

But what is it that these marks present to the viewer in their artful form? One answer is that they unearth a set of problems common to the immediacy of the loyalist youth's action and its conscious mimicry by the artist. For the loyalist, the mark is a defiant individual act in a toilet cubicle and an act of conformity in its suppression of individual difference. For the artist, the mark reveals an underlying complexity that muddies the transition from individual to social identity contained within the mark. Moreover, it is a complexity that cannot be readily articulated through the gestural act itself. To replicate this in the discursive and institutional confines of the modern gallery space is to undercut the idea of the centred subject and its expressive mark. All that remains in its wake is the idea of the artistic subject, caught amid the limits of linguistic convention and a fraught social structure, returning continually to the why of making.

*Gavin Murphy is a lecturer in Art History and Critical Theory at Galway-Mayo Institute of Technology.*

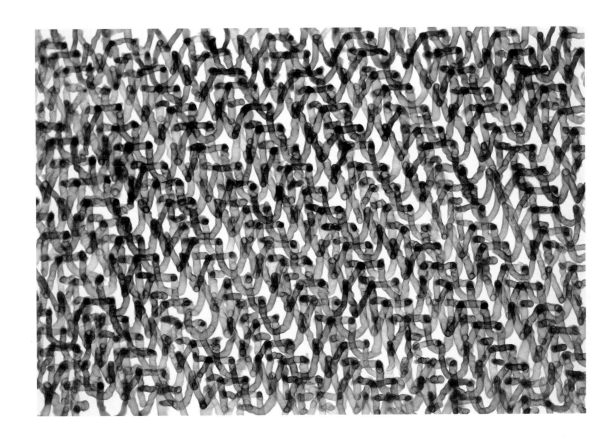

**Some of my friends are** 2004
Carbon, resin and gesso on wood
90 × 130 cm

*Ceiling Drawing* for Northern Ireland Exhibition,
Venice Biennale, 2005

**Ceiling Drawing**  2005
Carbon, resin and gesso on board

# Atul Dodiya

Atul Dodiya has lived and worked in Mumbai since his birth in 1959. He studied for a bachelor of fine arts at Sir J.J. School of Art, Bombay and Ecole des Beaux-Arts, Paris.

Past solo exhibitions of Dodiya's work have been shown at Fine Art Resource, Berlin, 2001, the Japan Foundation, Tokyo, 2001, and the Reina Sofia Museum, Madrid, 2002. He has also participated in numerous international group shows including the Venice Biennale 2005; the Yokohama Triennale 2001; *Edge of Desire: Recent Art in India* at the Art Gallery of Western Australia, Perth, which toured to New York, Mexico City, San Francisco and Toronto, 2004–06; *Tryst with Destiny: Art from Modern India*, Singapore Art Museum, Singapore, 1997; *Century City: Art & Culture in the Modern Metropolis Bombay/Mumbai*, Tate Modern, London, 2001; *Secular Practice; Recent Art from India*, Contemporary Art Gallery (CAG) Vancouver, 2002 and *Capital & Karma: Recent Position in Indian Art*, Kunsthalle, Vienna, 2002.

Dodiya had also received a number of awards which include the Gold Medal of Maharashtra Government, 1982, a fellowship at Sir J.J. School of Art, 1982, the Sanskriti Award, 1995, and the Sotheby's Prize, 1999. He was also awarded the French Government Scholarship, 1991–92, and the Civitella Ranieri Foundation Fellowship, Italy, 1999.

## Re-imagining Bapu

No project is more difficult to undertake for the contemporary Indian artist, perhaps, than that of representing a historical figure who dominated the recent past. Errors of judgement and the temptation to manufacture kitsch legend are among the attendant risks; and the scale of the difficulty can be imagined when the figure in question is a colossus like Mahatma Gandhi. Not only did the Mahatma live under the continuous glare of public attention, but his life has acquired a mythic dimension; arguably, there is no word, act, gesture, commitment or indecision of Gandhi's that has not been subjected to the posthumous encrustation of hagiography. Worse, the post-colonial India that was the outcome of Gandhi's struggle may have been a bitter disappointment to him; a realisation that probably informs, in some degree, India's rejection of his legacy of spiritual effort and social reformation.

This, nevertheless, is the task that Atul Dodiya set himself in the series of large watercolours entitled *An Artist of Non-violence*. The title is taken from one of Gandhi's own accounts, in which he implicitly accepts that the psychological motivation for his political activities is an aesthetic one: that of restoring balance, harmony and therefore beauty to a social formation, to human relationships and social institutions that had been thrown into disequilibrium by violent and tragic circumstances.

Dodiya regards the activity of painting as one of re-stating and improvising provisional resolutions around the puzzles placed before the us by the sphinx of history: among the themes that have occupied his paintings are the hiatus between preferred identity and given location, the mismatch between the object of attention and the images by which it is mediated into representational form. Given that such a tension informs Dodiya's art, it is appropriate that he should have taken Gandhi for the subject of his painterly contemplation; for the Mahatma too gathered creative energy from such a dialectic between contrary impulses.

As Indians, we cannot properly know ourselves without knowing the Mahatma. But it is his very familiarity that interposes a distance between ourselves and him: how shall we cut through the layers of preconception to reach the presence? The greatest difficulty is posed by the fact that Gandhi was a public figure in the most overwhelming sense of the term. His acts and thoughts were performed in the public sphere, deliberately exposed to the gaze of the mass media. He was a man who had no desire for privacy, who dramatised every detail of his inner life with a near obsessive honesty. Although this openness to scrutiny was not narcissistic but almost a religious observance: it was intended as a self-purification, which would prevent the ego from claiming him or insulating him against the heat and dust of world events.

Another layer of difficulty is generated by the ubiquity of Gandhi as an icon of the Republic. We are daily bombarded with fetishised images of the Father of the Nation: statues at traffic intersections and portraits in government offices, roads named after him, commemorative coins, stamps. And then there is the Gandhi of still photographs, newsreels and yellowed paper cuttings, replicated on stage and in film. Event has been enclosed in the shell of memory, and memory codified into narrative.

How does Dodiya release Gandhi from the stasis of these devices, how does he retrieve and re-imagine Bapu for us? In these watercolours we see a project of reclamation in progress, which aims to render the real presence of Gandhi, to honour the mystery that has successfully resisted the embalmer's hand. Dodiya's preoccupation with the document as a metaphor of history is also in evidence in these paintings, one of which is constructed as a bill for khadi sold, signed by Gandhi as seller and Dodiya as cashier. Elsewhere, too, the artist inscribes himself as a signatory to history by painting a page from the Mahatma's diary, collapsing past and present in a list of things to be done. Even the most momentous decisions and events, we realise, begin as stenographic notes jotted against a date; the imagination supplies the freight of circumstantial detail.

By tracing the cartography of Gandhi's mission in the scintillating manner that he has, Atul Dodiya has once again made Gandhi's personal heroism and his teachings palpable to us. The values that the Mahatma personified – the vigour of conviction, the responsibility of awareness, the nurturing or creativity and love – continue to be of crucial relevance to us today, and we ignore him at our own peril.

*An edited extract of the catalogue essay written by Ranjit Hoskote for Atul Dodiya's exhibition 'An Artist of Non-violence' at Gallery Chemould, Bombay, in 1999.*

**The Route to Dandi** 1998
Watercolour, marble dust and charcoal pencil on paper
172.7 × 111.7 cm
Private collection

**Sale of Khadi** 1998
Watercolour on paper
178 × 115 cm
Collection Galerie Mirchandani + Steinruecke, Mumbai

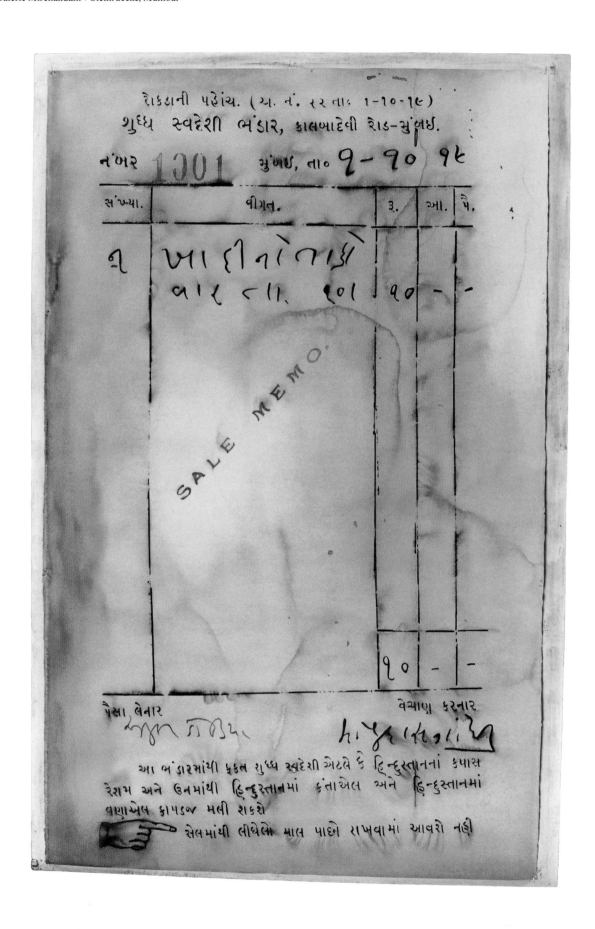

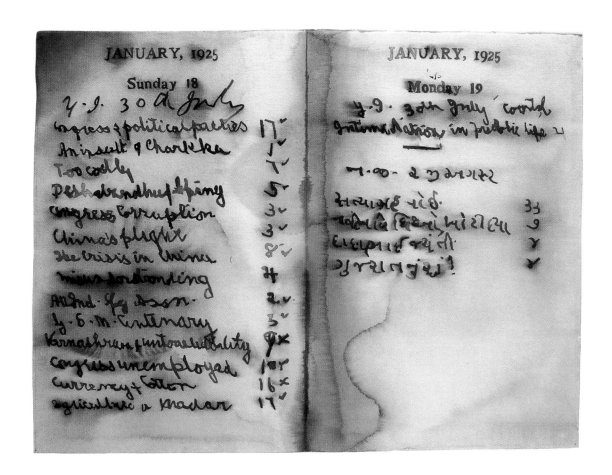

Seven singers. Seven songs. Each singer composed his/her own song. Some are survivors of massacres, others are witnesses to the horror that the drug war has brought to Colombia.

*Juan Manuel Echavarría*

# Juan Manuel Echavarría

Juan Manuel Echavarría was born in Medellín, Colombia in 1947. After 20 years as a novelist, Echavarría decided to become a photographer, and began making work about the violence in his country. As a writer, he had used metaphor to convey thoughts and feelings which had been difficult to describe but over time he had gradually become overwhelmed with words and so through photography and through metaphor he began to explore violence.

Echavarría has exhibited worldwide and his selected solo exhibitions include *Mouths of Ash*, which has been shown at a number of venues including the Americas Society, New York, 2006, North Dakota Museum of Art, USA, 2005, and Museo de Arte Moderno, Buenos Aires, 2000. His work has been shown in numerous group shows and film festivals including *The Disappeared* at El Centro Cultural Recoleta, Argentina, 2006, and North Dakota Museum of Art and the Venice Biennale, 2005; *The Hours: Visual Arts of Contemporary Latin America*, Irish Museum of Modern Art, 2005; San Francisco International film Festival, 2005; *Documentary Fortnight*, Museum of Modern Art, New York, 2005 and Toronto International Film Festival, 2004. Upcoming projects include a solo show at the Santa Fe Art Institute, 2007, and *The Disappeared* which will travel to venues including Museo de Arte de San Marcos, Lima, Peru, 2007, and The Museum of Modern Art, Bogotá, Colombia, 2008.

Echavarría lives and works in Bogotá, Colombia.

Luzmila Palacio

Oh Juradó, don't make me suffer anymore
Because I am dying of pain and I can't take it
any more [repeat]

In Juradó there wasn't time for sadness
Because its people were happy and cumbianvera
[repeat]

But war ended all the happiness
And the gas-can bombs closed the borders
[repeat]

Oh Juradó, don't make me suffer anymore
Because I am dying of pain and I can't take it
any more [repeat]

In Colombia, the exodus is massive
Children are not respected nor the elderly
[repeat]

The old man is left forgotten
And we the poor are treated with horror [repeat]

Oh Juradó, don't make me suffer anymore
Because I am dying of pain and I can't take it
any more [repeat]

You are rich because you have oxygen
Your wood and also your folklore [repeat]

Biodiversity in all the species
Of fauna that were left to us by the Lord [repeat]

Oh Juradó, don't make me suffer anymore
Because I am dying of pain and I can't take it
any more [repeat]

"Ay Juradó no me hagas mar sufrir
que me muero de dolor y no puedo resistir"
(bis)

en Juradó no había tiempo de tristeza
toda su gente era alegre y cumbianbera
(bis)

pero la guerra acabo con la alegría
y los cilindros cerraron la frontera (bis)

"Ay Juradó no me hagas mar sufrir
que me muero de dolor y no puedo resistir"
(bis)

En Colombia el éxodo es masivo
no se respeta al niño, ni al mayor... (bis)

Al anciano lo echan al olvido
y a los pobres nos tratan con horror (bis)

"Ay Juradó no me hagas mar sufrir
que me muero de dolor y no puedo resistir"
(bis)

Tu eres rico porque tienes oxigeno
tu madera y también por tu folclor... (bis)

Biodiverso en todas las especies...
de la fauna que nos dejo el Señor... (bis)

"Ay Juradó no me hagas mar sufrir
que me muero de dolor y no puedo resistir"
(bis)

**Bocas de Ceniza / Mouths of Ash**  2003–04
Video still and lyrics

Nacer Hernández

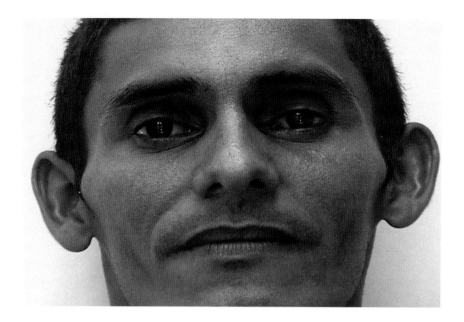

**Two Brothers (Part one of duet)**

I am going to tell you a sad story
The one that happened to us
Where many people died
And that is what causes me pain

It was February 10th
When my brother and I
Were that day going on leave
But a son of the devil accused us there

Saying we were guerrillas
As if to gain honour
But since we are with God
And because we are with God we are here again

Oh life! You have to pay attention to life
Because life is full of mysteries
That night I had a dream
Where the Lord revealed to me
A ship covered in black
That maybe was my casket
But then I remembered
And prayed to the Lord for me and my family

You most distance yourself from Lucifer
Because those were things of envy

And since we have faith in the Lord
And since we have faith in the Lord
We ask him for a long life
Since we have faith in the Lord
Since we have faith in the Lord
We ask him for a long life

We ask him for a long life
Since we have faith in the Lord
Since we have faith in the Lord
We ask him to give us long life

**Dos Hermanos (Parte 1 del dúo)**

Voy a contarles una triste historia
la que a nosotros nos sucedió
donde muchas personas murieron.
Y eso es lo que me da dolor.

Eso fue un 10 de febrero
donde se encontraba mi hermano y yo
ese día iba a ir de relevo
pero un hijo del diablo nos acusó.

Aaaay... diciendo que éramos guerrilleros
como para ganar honor
pero como estamos con Dios
y como estamos con Dios, estamos aquí de nuevo.

A la vida hay que pararle bolas
porque la vida esta llena de misterio.
Esa noche yo tuve un sueño
Y el que el Señor me reveló
una embarcación cubierta de negro
que quizá era mi cajón
pero enseguida recordé
y le pedí a Dios por mí, por mi familia.

Hay que apartar a Lucifer
porque ésas eran cosas de la envidia... (bis)

Y como al Señor le tenemos fe
y como le tenemos fe le pedimos larga vida
le pedimos larga vida
como al Señor le tenemos fe
como al Señor le tenemos fe
le pedimos larga vida.

le pedimos larga vida
como al Señor le tenemos fe
como al Señor le tenemos fe
le pedimos larga vida

**Dorismel Hernández**

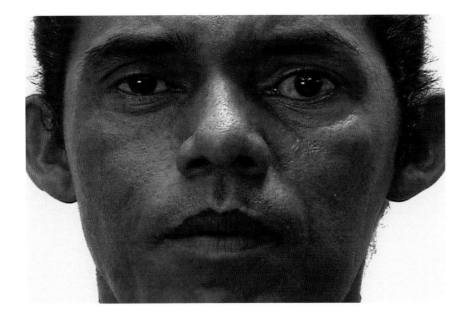

**Two Brothers (Part two of duet)**

Lord, you saved my life
When I most needed you
And now once again I have to continue with it
And give, give you my soul

To give you all my caring
To give you all my love
And that you light my path
To follow, to follow you my Lord

Because to me you are the most beautiful thing
I want to enter into your heart
I also want to be one of your children
To distance, distance myself from pain

I want to live to sing to you Lord
I want to live to make you happy

When I was handcuffed, was tied up
I prayed to you for my brother and me
And at that moment you were listening to me
And that is what makes me so happy

Oh, when they were massacring, when they were killing
I felt, I felt like crying
I only prayed to you, my God up in heaven
That you would save us, and nothing would happen to us

But your weapon was more powerful
That those that were sent by Satan

Because even with all the killing
My brother and I were saved

I want to live to sing to you, Jehovah
I want to live to make you happy, Lord
I want to live to make you happy, Lord
I want to live to make you happy

**Dos Hermanos (Parte 2 del dúo)**

¡Señor! Tú que me salvaste la vida
cuando yo más te necesitaba
y ahora de nuevo tengo que seguirla
y entregarte, entregarte mi alma.

Entregarte todo mi cariño
entregarte todo mi amor…
y que me ilumines el camino
para seguirte, seguirte Señor

Porque para mí, tú eres lo más lindo
yo quiero entrar en tu corazón
yo también quiero ser uno de tus hijos…
para apartarme, apartarme del dolor.

Quiero vivir para cantarte, Señor,
quiero vivir para alegrarte.

Cuando yo estaba esposado, estaba atado,
te pedí por mi hermano y por mí…
y en ese momento me estabas escuchando,
y eso es lo que me tiene tan feliz.

Aaaay… cuando estaban masacrando, que estaban matando…
sentía ganas, ganas de llorar,
sólo te pedí a ti, mi Dios del cielo,
que nos salvaras y no nos pasara nada.

Pero tu arma fue más poderosa
que aquélla que había mandao Satanás.

Porque a pesar de tanta matanza
mi hermano y yo nos pudimos salvar… (bis)

Quiero vivir para cantarte, Jehová,
quiero vivir para alegrarte, Señor,
quiero vivir para alegrarte, Señor,
quiero vivir para alegrarte

# David Farrell

David Farrell was born in Dublin in 1961. He read chemistry at University College Dublin, graduating with a PhD in 1987. He has worked as a freelance photographer since 1990 and on 'communion' projects with his partner, the writer Gogo della Luna (Gudók). His work has been exhibited at Fotofest, Houston, 2006; Iwate Museum of Art, Japan, 2005; Festival Internazionale di Fotografia at Museum of Rome, 2005; Glasgow Museum of Modern Art, 2003, and the International BACKLIGHT Festival, Tampere, Finland, 2002. He received the European Publishers' Award for Photography in 2001 for *Innocent Landscapes* and in 2004 participated in the *European Eyes on Japan* project. *Crow*, his collaborative multimedia film with composer Benjamin Dwyer, was premiered during the Composers' Choice Festival at the National Concert Hall Dublin in 2005. He is currently being filmed for a documentary by Donald Taylor Black (Poolbeg Productions).

At present he lives in Dublin where he works as a lecturer in photography at the Dun Laoghaire Institute for Art, Design and Technology.

**Innocent Landscapes, Oristown (Twilight)** 1999
Colour photograph
107 × 107 cm

## Innocent Landscapes

In 30 years of conflict and atrocity in Northern Ireland a small group of people stood apart: they were the 'missing', the 'disappeared' – absent and yet somehow still present. Even their exact number was uncertain, though it was thought that there were at least 15 people whose whereabouts had remained shrouded in misinformation and doubt since the 1970s and early 1980s. Despite considerable obfuscation it was considered that their fate and whereabouts was directly linked to what was colloquially known as the Troubles. Apart from Capt. Robert Nairac, an undercover British soldier, they were all Catholic and widely assumed to have been 'disappeared' by the IRA through a process of internal policing of the movement and the wider catholic community. What separated this group from other 'policings' was the silence, the denial and the absence of a body for uncertain relatives. This renunciation continued for over 25 years.

On 29 March 1999 as a result of the ongoing peace process, the IRA issued a statement in which they apologised and accepted the 'injustice of prolonging the suffering of victim's families' and admitted what they termed 'the killing and secret burial' of 10 people. Despite internal enquiries they had only managed to locate the burial places of nine people: Bryan McKinney, John McClory, Danny McIlhone, Brendan Megraw, Jean McConville, Kevin McKee, Seamus Wright, Columba McVeigh and Eamonn Molloy.

The locations – Colgagh, Ballynultagh, Oristown, Templetown, Wilkinstown, Bragan, and Faughart – contained a simple but final bitter twist: they were all located in the Republic of Ireland. This small group of people had been exiled in death creating a poignant and, as time progressed, haunting 'diaspora of the disappeared'. This became evident when, on 20 May 2000, the digs, now in their second phase, were suspended: three remains had been located, three closures permitted, leaving the remaining families with a site rather than a spot, a closing rather than a closure.*

My initial response upon visiting my first site at Colgagh was visceral. It was some weeks after the discovery of the remains of Bryan McKinney and John McClory and there was 'nothing' to photograph. Well, certainly nothing in a conventional documentary mode, however the violated landscape jarred me. It seemed to be a powerful metaphor for the violence that had taken place there over 20 years ago that only now had become visible by the scarification of the land during the search process – I left thinking 'they must be made to see'. Somehow this small group of people epitomised the complexities of political violence – where a society becomes so brutalised that it starts to murder its own in the pursuit of the 'rights' of its people.

There was a also a thread that connected most of the sites, both topographically and somewhat conceptually to the nature of photography itself. A link that is in many ways an essence of the Irish landscape – the bog, that memory bank, that witness of history and trauma. The writer Terry Eagleton has commented on the bog as revealing 'the past as still present' and that objects contained within them are 'caught in a living death'. *Innocent Landscapes* – like many works that deal with violence and commemoration and in particular those that are by default utilising what has been termed as 'late photography' – contains a number of dilemmas. How do you photograph something that was intended to remain unseen? How do you photograph something where the referent, which in photography is normally carried forward to any future, has been completely removed from the *mise-en-scene*, where the experiences undergone by the disappeared were meant to be outside of memory and denied to those who experienced them? How do you photograph 'nothing' in the hope that it will trigger a response? How do you photograph 'the intangible presence of absence'?

As I began to visit these sites I was struck by their beauty. They were so typical of classical representations of the Irish landscape in painting, cinema and even within the commercial world of tourism – they exuded a rich symbol of what in some ways it means to be Irish. At first this beauty issue troubled me. Would it be possible to essentially aestheticise violence in a meaningful way? Could I usurp this beauty and turn it back against itself? Early on within the work a chance meeting with Mrs McKinney (mother of Bryan), where she commented that 'she had felt a sense of relief when Bryan had been found with nature in such a beautiful place', made me realize that location of place, for an absent memory and an intense loss, would be a key element in my excavation of these sites and that an inherent almost romantic beauty somehow acted as a comfort cloak of reflection. I was aware that I was possibly questioning the medium's ability to not only furnish evidence but also the limits it placed on remembering, representing and commemorating traumatic historical events. In the end all I felt I could do was bear witness in order to make the viewer bear witness to what was essentially a framed absence.

As time passed and nature began to reclaim these locations, making them disappear from immediate consciousness, it comforted me to some extent that my involvement with these sites and the people said to be buried there was not a completely futile artistic gesture of protest in that my photographs would exist as a monument of sorts, an act of remembrance in the face of voracious nature, human forgetfulness and the folly of memory.

*David Farrell*

* Since the publication of Innocent Landscapes the earth itself returned Jean McConville at a location approximately 500m from the excavated site when the shifting sands of the beach revealed her remains to a man out walking his dog in August 2003. A resumed search was also carried out to no avail for Columba McVeigh at Bragan in September 2003.

**Innocent Landscapes, Ballynultagh** 2000
Colour photograph
107 × 152 cm

**Innocent Landscapes, Oristown / Templetown** 2000, 1999
Colour photographs, diptych
82 × 164 cm

# Shilpa Gupta

Shilpa Gupta was born in Mumbai, India in 1976.
Between 1992–97, she studied sculpture at the
Sir J.J. School of Fine Arts, Mumbai. Gupta creates
artwork using interactive websites, video, gallery
environments and public perfomances to probe and
examine subversively such themes as consumer
culture, exploitation of labour, militarism and human
rights abuse.

Gupta has exhibited internationally and recent shows
include the Sydney Biennale 2006; Liverpool Biennale
2006, Havana Biennial 2006; ICC Tokyo 2005;
*Edge of Desire: Recent Art in India*, New York, 2005;
Fukuoka Asian Art Triennale 2005 and Media City
Seoul Biennale 2004. She has also worked on many
online art projects including *Blessed Bandwidth.net*,
2005, an on-line art project commissioned for Tate
Online and her upcoming projects include the Lyon
Biennale 2007. She has received a number of awards
including International Artist of the Year, South
Asian Visual Artists Collective, Canada, 2004;
Transmediale 2004 Award, Berlin and Sanskriti
Prathisthan Award, New Delhi, 2004.

Gupta currently lives and works in Mumbai.

In this wall projection, are seven figures, all dressed up in the *camouflage* – which has become increasingly fashionable after the War on Terror Campaign. First in the West, and more recently, spilling East onto the streets outside my home. Now I can walk into shops two blocks from where I live and buy camouflage gear. Camouflage makes you feel *Cool* and masquerade Terror. Terror is quite *Cool*.

Click on the figures and they move, they copy, they imitate. Click one, click two, choose a leader, become a leader and the rest follow. If they stop, click them up and they join. Exercise 1 – 2 – 3 – 4. One Bend, Two Bend, Three Bend, Stay. Look Straight – Don't See – STAY

I have a bag, I have a phone, my neighbour has a phone, my phone, I don't have a phone, I don't have a shopping bag, but I need to JOG for it. Jog Jog Jog Stay on the Spot. Jog Jog Stay Stay

March Free Speech Free Press Free Market March Market Market March Free Speech No Speech No Press Market Market Market March March

Shut and Be. Shut and Eat. Don't Interrupt. PRAY. Fun Merry Merry Merry Fun Fun. DO or OUT. Aim 1234 Right Kill 1234 Left Aim 1234 Shoot Shoot Aim Shoot 1234 1234 1234 4,4

Dumb-ed in a capitalist society, we enjoy being programmed. We find instant satiation and loss of memory in turning ourselves into puppets. We allow media, electronic extensions of ourselves now in hands of a corporate often with state support nexus to think for us and amputate individual reasoning (McLuhan). Mental and physical activity slips from the mechanical to the mindless deteriorating into fear, chaos

and violence against an enemy does not exist in a world where global consent is hijacked to fight a war in search of weapons which were never there. Everybody Bend; Dont Talk, Dont See, Dont Hear. Gandhi said so.

The project recalls a psychology where a combination of healthy physical exercises can help in slow and intense indoctrination of the mind by intense State military drills, local Hindu right wing RSS cadre exercises or new age courses to make you fighting fit.

The interactive loop keeps slipping into mindless violence. Violence – which is no longer just a fashion but is being internalized, morphing the emptied vulnerable self to become a source to project it towards the State, which is no longer the sole entity that has monopoly over the legitimate use of violence.

*Shilpa Gupta*

# Alia Hasan-Khan

Alia Hasan-Khan was born in 1970 in Rawalpindi,
Pakistan, and in 1994 achieved a bachelor of fine art
at the Indus Valley School of Art & Architecture in
Karachi, Pakistan. In 1998, she received a master of
fine art from Tufts University/School of the Museum
of Fine Arts, Boston, USA.

Hasan-Khan is interested in maintaining her practice
in both Pakistan and North America and her work
engages and reflects upon the social and political
issues surrounding both of these areas.

Recent selected exhibitions include *Outside the
Cube* and *Homecoming* at the National Art Gallery,
Islamabad, Pakistan, 2007; *Subcontingent*, Fondazione
Sandretto Re Rebaudengo, Torino, Italy, and *When
Artists Say We*, Artists Space, New York, 2006.

My work engages with social and political issues in direct and palpable ways. I believe that art practice is most interesting when it is both topical and timeless. I see this practice like a journalist or a writer expressing an opinion, suggesting an idea, or presenting another way of looking through visual means. Site specifically, the work deals with issues around the place I live.

In *Kidnapped: homage to Karachi*, I present the hapless perspective of a bound person laying in the back seat of a car as s/he is driven through the streets of Karachi. Like many mega-cities throughout the world where there is huge disparity in wealth, kidnappings of the elite classes have become a common occurrence in Karachi. Many of these kidnappings are undertaken by young men from the middle classes (who are often well-connected within the police and judiciary) who see this 'profession' as the only means to access the decadent consumerist culture of the elites. This video also evokes attitudes pervasive in a city that has seen much chaos and violence in the past 20 years. The two protagonists, in their casual conversation about prices of food and where to eat lunch, reflect a fearless and cynical position towards their crime, even attempting to crack a few jokes during their journey.

*Alia Hasan-Khan*

overleaf:
**Kidnapped: homage to Karachi** 2004
Video stills

# Alfredo Jaar

Alfredo Jaar, born in 1956, is a Chilean artist, architect and filmmaker who now lives and works in New York. His work has been exhibited in solo and group shows in museums and galleries around the world, including the New Museum of Contemporary Art, New York, 2003; the Whitechapel Gallery, London, 1992; Museum of Contemporary Art, Chicago, 1992; the Pergamon Museum, Berlin, 1992 and the Fotografiska Museet, Moderna Museet, Stockholm, 1994. Jaar has also displayed work at bienniales in Brighton, 2006, Canarias, 2006, Sevilla, 2006, Johannesburg, 1997, Kwangju, 1995, Istanbul, 1995, Sydney, 1990, São Paulo, 1987, Venice, 1986 as well as Documenta XI, Kassel, 2002. He received a Guggenheim Fellowship in 1985 and was made a MacArthur Fellow in 2000.

Jaar dedicated six years to *The Rwanda Project*, 1994–2000. His new project, *Muxima*, 2005, focuses on Angola and has been exhibited at the Reina Sofia, Madrid, 2006, the Fundacion Tapies, Barcelona, 2006, and the Centre Pompidou, Paris, 2007. It will be shown at the 2007 Venice Biennale.

A major anthology, 'La Politique des Images,' opens in May 2007 at the Musee des Beaux Arts in Lausanne.

April 6, 1994: A plane carrying the presidents of Rwanda and Burundi is shot down above Kigali, the capital of Rwanda. Their deaths spark widespread massacres, targeting Hutu moderates and the minority Tutsi population, in Kigali and throughout Rwanda. The Rwandan Patriotic Front, which had been encamped along the northern border of Rwanda, starts a new offensive.

April 6, 1994: A plane carrying the presidents of Rwanda and Burundi is shot down above Kigali, the capital of Rwanda. Their deaths spark widespread massacres, targeting Hutu moderates and the minority Tutsi population, in Kigali and throughout Rwanda. The Rwandan Patriotic Front, which had been encamped along the northern border of Rwanda, starts a new offensive.

April 12, 1994: The interim Rwandan government flees Kigali for the town of Gitarama. Relief officials estimate that as many as 25,000 people have been killed in Kigali alone in the first five days of violence.

April 21, 1994: The United Nations Security Council Resolution 912 reduces the UN peacekeeping force in Rwanda from 2,500 to 270. 50,000 deaths.

April 30, 1994: At least 1.3 million Rwandans have fled their homes. More than 250,000 refugees cross the border into Tanzania, the largest mass exodus ever witnessed by the United Nations High Commissioner for Refugees. 100,000 deaths.

May 8, 1994: The Rwandan Patriotic Front gains control of most of northern Rwanda. As killings continue, hundreds of thousands of refugees flee to Zaire, Burundi and Uganda. 200,000 deaths.

May 13, 1994: More than 30,000 bodies wash down the Kagera River, which marks Rwanda's border with Tanzania.

May 17, 1994: The United Nations Security Council passes Resolution 918 authorizing the deployment of 5,500 UN troops to Rwanda. The resolution says: "acts of genocide may have been committed."

May 22, 1994: The Rwandan Patriotic Front gains full control of Kigali and the airport. 300,000 deaths.

May 26, 1994: Deployment of the mainly African UN force is delayed due to a dispute over who will provide equipment and cover the cost for the operation. 400,000 deaths.

June 5, 1994: The United States argues with the UN over the cost of providing heavy armored vehicles for the peacekeeping force. 500,000 deaths.

June 10, 1994: The killing of Tutsis and moderate Hutus continues, even in refugee camps. 600,000 deaths.

June 17, 1994: France announces its plan to send 2,500 troops to Rwanda as an interim peacekeeping force until the UN troops arrive. 700,000 deaths.

June 22, 1994: With still no sign of UN deployment, the United Nations Security Council authorizes the deployment of 2,500 French troops in southwest Rwanda. 800,000 deaths.

June 28, 1994: The UN Rights Commission's special envoy releases a report stating that the massacres were pre-planned and formed part of a systematic campaign of genocide.

July 4, 1994: French troops establish a so-called "safe zone" in the southwest of Rwanda.

July 8, 1994: As the Rwandan Patriotic Front advances westward, the influx of displaced persons into the so-called "safe zone" increases from 500,000 to 1 million within a few days. 900,000 deaths.

July 12, 1994: An estimated 1.5 million Rwandans flee toward Zaire. More than 15,000 refugees cross the border every hour and enter the town of Goma, which becomes the largest refugee camp in the world. A cholera epidemic sweeps through the camps in and around Goma, killing an estimated 50,000 people more.

July 21, 1994: The United Nations Security Council reaches a final agreement to send an international force to Rwanda. One million people have been killed. Two million have fled the country. Another two million are displaced within Rwanda.

August 1, 1994: Newsweek magazine dedicates its first *ever* cover to Rwanda.

*Alfredo Jaar*
*Text from 'Untitled (Newsweek)', 1994*

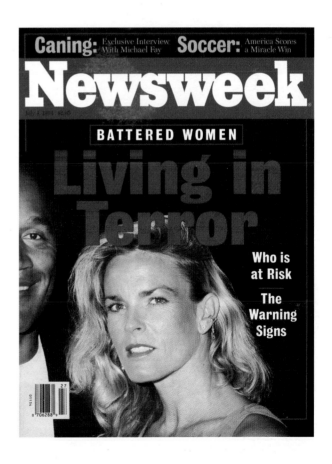

**Untitled (Newsweek)** 1994
Texts and digital prints of front covers of Newsweek magazine

June 28, 1994: The UN Rights Commission's special envoy releases a report stating that the massacres were pre-planned and formed part of a systematic campaign of genocide.
June 4, 1994: French troops establish a so-called "safe zone" in the southwest of Rwanda.

**Untitled (Newsweek)** 1994
Texts and digital prints of front covers of Newsweek magazine

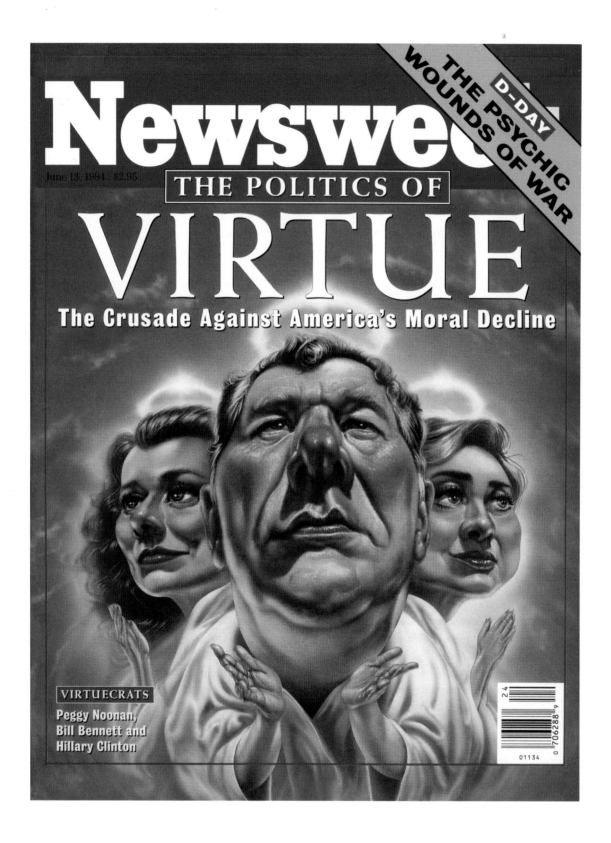

**June 10, 1994:** The killing of Tutsis and moderate Hutus continues, even in refugee camps. 600,000 deaths.

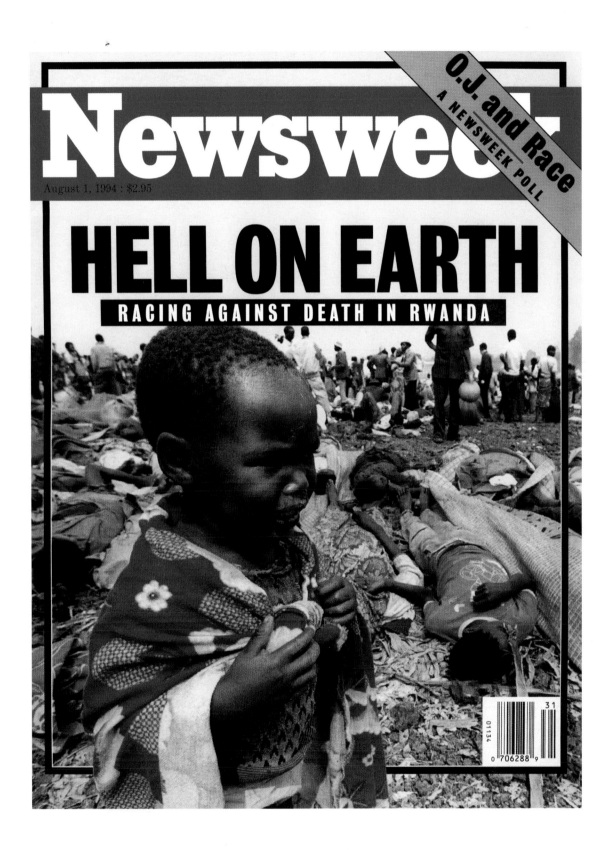

**Newsweek**

August 1, 1994 : $2.95

**HELL ON EARTH**

**RACING AGAINST DEATH IN RWANDA**

O.J. and Race
A NEWSWEEK POLL

**August 1, 1994:** Newsweek magazine dedicates its first cover to Rwanda.

# Jitish Kallat

Jitish Kallat was born in 1974 in Mumbai, India, where he now lives and works. He received his bachelor of fine art in painting from the Sir J.J. School of Art, Mumbai in 1996 where he became a fellow in 1997.

Kallat has had solo shows at Gallery Chemould, Mumbai, Nature Morte, New Delhi, Bodhi Art, Singapore, Bose Pacia Modern, New York, Walsh Gallery, Chicago and Gallery Barry Keldoulis, Sydney among others. Forthcoming solo shows include Arario Beijing and Albion Gallery, London, 2007.

Kallat has participated in numerous exhibitions including the *Thermocline Of Art*, ZKM Museum, Karlsruhe, 2007; Gwangju Biennale 2006; Asia Pacific Triennale 2006, Brisbane; Lille 3000, 2006; *Passages*, Palais De Beaux Arts, Brussels, 2006; *Another Worlds*, Arario Gallery, Cheonan, Korea, 2006; *Indian Summer*, Ecole de Beaux Arts, Paris, 2005; *Armory Show*, New York, 2005; *Zoom*, Culturgest Museum, Lisbon, 2004; *Subterrain*, HKW, Berlin, 2004; *The Tree From The Seed*, Henie Onstad Kultursenter, Oslo, 2003; *Under Construction*, Japan Foundation Asia Center, Tokyo, 2002; *Century City*, Tate Modern, London, 2001; Havana Biennial 2000; Fukuoka Asian Art Triennale 1999, Fukuoka, Japan; *Art of the World 1998*, Passage de Retz, Paris, and *Innenseite*, Kassel, 1997.

As I write this short note about two of my works, *The Lie of The Land*, 2004, and *Cenotaph (A Deed of Transfer)*, 2007, an assortment of current events might be worth recounting.

Last week, a group of right-wing activists ransacked an art school in Baroda and arrested a young student for allegedly hurting religious sentiments with his paintings. While the dean of the art school was unfairly suspended, the rioting political workers, now omnipresent in the violent mobocracy of the Indian state, heroically declared the codes of morality to a desperate, sound-byte-seeking media. Elsewhere, in Punjab, two separate sects of the Sikh community have been killing each other for the last two days and a bomb erupted in a mosque in Hyderabad just four hours ago. As the news spread, Mumbai is witnessing stone pelting and burning of buses in response to the Hyderabad bomb blast.

The scrap-happy media breaks the news while the perpetrators of violence break the law and carry out their action, often occasioned to catch the prime-time audience.

In the portfolio of drawings titled *The Lie of the Land*, images as varied as those of rioters and that of a leading Indian politician feeding a cow at a well planned photo-op, are sourced from the pop poop of the media, evoking violence, pain, greed and power. The fluid black and white drawings are blown through a vacuum cleaner while the painting is still in process. In doing so, I re-enact the role of the perpetrator/ gunman administering the drawing with a veneer of violence and the work undergoes a significant transformation of meaning.

The photo work titled *Cenotaph (A Deed Of Transfer)* was conceived after I witnessed a demolition drive conducted on a squatter settlement alongside a pavement in Mumbai. These were brick homes built against a wall that separates the railway tracks from a parallel road called the Tulsi Pipe Road. To see the (albeit illegal) homes being ruthlessly and somewhat violently pulled down was indeed a ghastly sight.

A few weeks later, while passing on the same road I observed that the homes were gone and their residents had fled. The supporting wall against which these houses were built had been reabsorbed back as a city wall and slowly film posters and advertising bills were being pasted on them. I began documenting these walls. They carried several traces of domestic life in the form of wall tiles, leftovers of electric wiring, clothes, calendars, images of deities, etc. I decided to work through the images such that, in the 3-D lenticular format every element in the photograph and every residue of aggression gets activated and levitates in mid-air as if they were vengeful festoons holding up the memory of the tragic demolition.

The work addresses a kind of violence that has social sanction and passes approvingly as part of daily governance. It foregrounds traces of the assault engraved on the homes as symbolic of another kind of violence; that of the progressive India (referred to as 'India Shining' in election campaigns and as 'Incredible India' in tourist brochures) which ruthlessly ignores or eradicates every eyesore in its field of vision. The squatter community on the streets of Mumbai is once such example.

On a personal front, I see *Cenotaph (A Deed of Transfer)* as images I dispatch into the world as self-addressed envelopes that carry the message into the world but also back to the self.

*Jitish Kallat*
*May 2007*
*Mumbai*

**Cenotaph (A Deed of Transfer)** 2007
Lenticular prints
44.5 × 66 cm

**Cenotaph (A Deed of Transfer)** 2007
Lenticular prints
44.5 × 66 cm

**52**

**The Lie of the Land**  2004
Mixed media work on handmade paper
71.1 × 106.7 cm
Courtesy of Walsh Gallery, Chicago

# Amar Kanwar

Amar Kanwar's recent exhibitions include the Sydney Biennale, 2006; *Image War: Contesting Images Of Political Conflict*, ISP Exhibition, Whitney Museum, New York, 2006; Lofoten International Art Exhibition, Norway, 2006; *Sub-contingent*, Fondazione Sandretto Re Rebaudengo, Turin, Italy, 2006; *Experiments with Truth*, Fabric Workshop Museum, Philadelphia, 2005 and *Patriot*, Baltimore Museum of Contemporary Art, USA, 2005.

Recent solo exhibitions have been shown at the APJ Media Gallery, New Delhi, 2007; National Museum of Art, Oslo, 2006; Fotogalleriet, Oslo, 2005; Tensta Konsthall, Stockholm, 2003, and The Renaissance Society, Chicago, 2003. Kanwar has also participated in *Historical Retrospective – 50 years of Oberhausen*, Germany, 2004; the 10th Biennial of Moving Images, Museum of Modern and Contemporary Art, Geneva, 2003; Fri-Art Centre d'art Contemporain Kunsthalle, Switzerland, 2003; KalaGhoda Art Festival, Mumbai, 2002; *Other India's – Breaking the Code*, Whitechapel Art Gallery, London, 2002; Werkleitz Biennale, Germany, 2002 and Documenta XI, Kassel, 2002.

He is also the recipient of the first Edvard Munch Award for Contemporary Art, Norway, 2005; Honorary Doctorate in Fine Arts, Maine College of Art, USA, 2006; First Prize, Torino International Film Festival, Italy, 2002; Grand Prix, EnviroFilm, Slovakia, 2002; Golden Gate Award, San Francisco International Film Festival, 2002, 2001 and 1998; Jury's Award, Film South Asia, Nepal, 2000; MacArthur Fellowship, India, 2000 and the Golden Conch Award, Mumbai International Film Festival, 1998.

Kanwar is currently working on a project entitled *The Torn First Pages*, a series of short and long films that emerge from the democracy movement in Burma and a new work relating to the submerging of narratives in political conflicts which is to be presented at Documenta XII in Kassel, Germany, 2007.

Kanwar lives and works in New Delhi, India.

There is, perhaps, no border outpost in the world quite like Wagah, where this film begins its exploration. An outpost where every evening people are drawn to a thin white line. Probably anyone in the eye of a conflict could find themselves here.

Emerging from the Indian subcontinent, the film is a contemporary narrative that connects intimate personal spheres of existence to larger socio-political processes. Linking legends and ritual objects to new symbols and public events, it maps an exploration of our relationship with the politics of power, violence, sexuality and justice.

*Amar Kanwar*

**A Season Outside** 1997
Video still

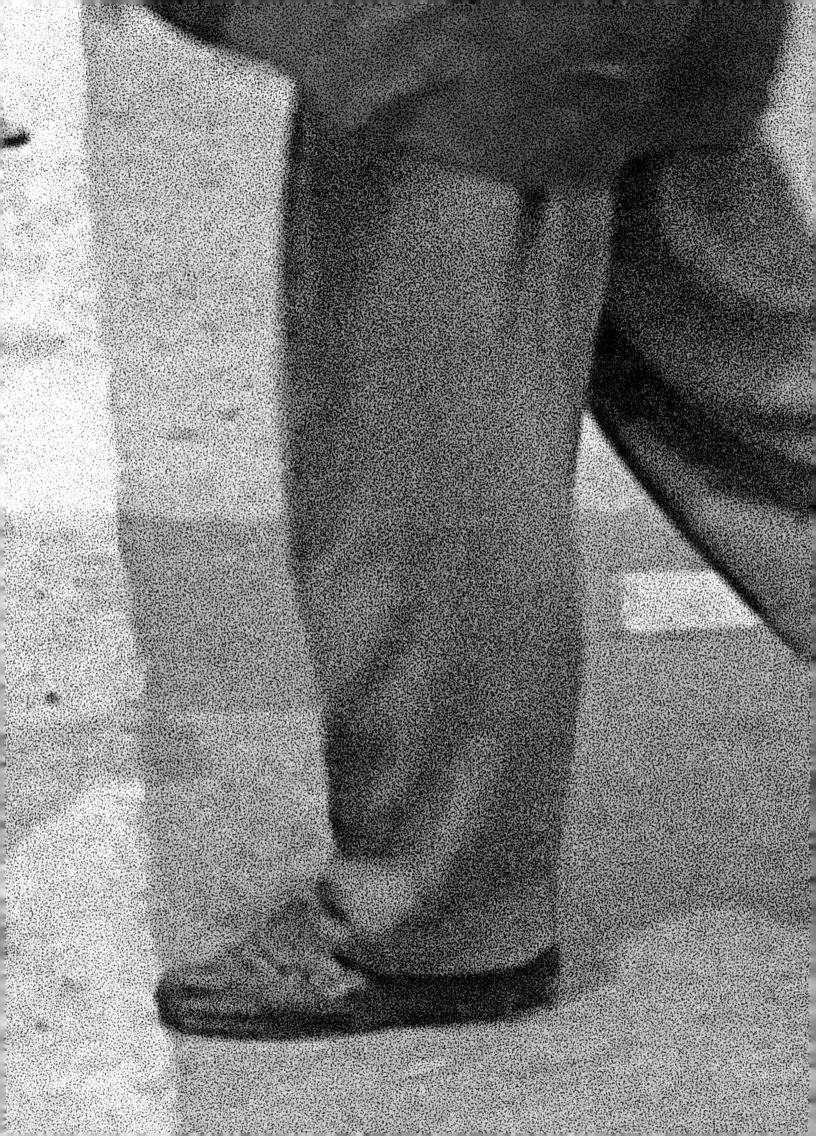

# Dave Lewis

Dave Lewis was born in England in 1962. He attended the Polytechnic of Central London (now University of Westminster) to study film and photography in the mid-1980s and later worked for the community-based Blackfriars Photography Project in south east London. Lewis's work has appeared in a number of publications around themes of race, identity and representation. His work *Untitled (Royal Anthropological Institute, London)*, 1995, was incorporated into the Arts Council Collection in 2001. He has exhibited widely in solo and group shows including The Photographers' Gallery, London; MOMA, Oxford; Recontres d'Arles, France.

Lewis has continued working as a commercial photographer and gives talks and workshops in galleries and schools, as well as lecturing in further and higher education institutions. Lewis is currently working on projects around three areas: mental health, urban issues and anthropology where he is currently a visiting research fellow in the Department of Anthropology at Goldsmiths, University of London. He is a member of the Bermondsey Artists Group.

Lewis lives and works in London.

As I write this it has been almost 14 years since the murder of Stephen Lawrence and eight years since the publication by the Home Office in 1999 of the McPherson Report or, as I prefer to call it, quoting The Right Reverend Dr. John Sentamu, now Archbishop Sentamu, the Stephen Lawrence Report. The stark reality is the Home Office version of the case (a report that demands authority) will be entombed in official literature for future generations long after newspaper reports, related documents, oral accounts and indeed books have become supporting material and footnotes filed in future archival systems. I want to be clear about my position in this: in my mind justice has not been done. The report has left a legacy of bitterness and a smouldering feeling of resentment that I suspect will be passed down through the blood to many future generations of black men and women as a defining moment of being black in Britain at the end of the 20th century. In my mind it stands as a marker of race relations along with the riots in Brixton (and nationwide) and the still 'unsolved' teenage deaths in the Deptford fire in 1981. The residue of conflict seeps through bodies and minds. This, I think, is the *AfterShock* that the inclusion of my work attends to.

Just as civil servants in the Home Office had edited the Stephen Lawrence Report to a shortened version, I have edited *Chapter Six – Racism* to bring my own mind's-eye vision of the report, albeit with artistic licence. I have tried to use the text creatively (although not too creatively as there are strict rules about this) to tell a story of a black man within his personal space, coming to terms with the report and hopefully delivering to the viewer the idea that discrimination affects us psychologically and continuously, and follows us into our private space. The text is used less as an anchor and more as background speech: as you look at the pictures imagine the voice of news reports on Radio 4.

And what of the police? Well, this morning a new publication by a high-ranking officer who is an Iranian Muslim and is obviously very unhappy about his treatment by 'his own' is being reported on and, on Radio 4, serialised. The recent shooting of suspected terrorist Jean Charles de Menezes had brought concern about police anti-terrorist activities to the fore (i.e. to middle England) with, bizarrely, a promotion of one of the senior officers responsible for the operation that went so badly wrong. There has been a dramatic increase in teenagers carrying and using knives and fire-arms with deadly intent and effect, even with the existence of a specialist police unit, Trident, to tackle gun crime in London's black communities. However, there has also been a notable increase of community police officers, perhaps not such a bad thing, although I'm unclear if the police forces around London have the same view.

Why am I going on about all this? For me it goes to context. The context is the social and political environment in which conflict on either domestic or international scale is managed. I would like to say that if conflict is managed through debate and analysis with pertinent and direct action exercised in individual cases, then wider social conflict will be managed in the same way, hopefully avoiding repeat situations. But I sense I am wrong. What I witness now is a different ethnic group protesting about arbitrary and unfair treatment at the hands of the police and, by proxy, the state. To be brutally honest it gives me an opportunity to drive past slowly to see how it feels to be target-free (false, as it happens, as I too have been stopped as part of 'terrorist checks'). A young Muslim woman who I was teaching was telling me how she felt just walking into her local tube station. She made sure her Oyster pass was out and ready. She felt that she was always being watched and didn't want to give 'them' the excuse to stop her and ask her a range of questions which had nothing to do with how much credit she did or did not have on her Oyster pass.

And we're back at the beginning. Perhaps another narrative-based piece in photographic or other form will look again more critically at race relations at the beginning of the 21st century. Perhaps it's mindless to even think that anything can be changed by displaying two or three-dimensional objects (or moving images) within an internal shifting space named gallery or museum. But I do want you to know that during the past 14 years, probably the past 14 centuries and the centuries to come, that I and others (hundreds, thousands, millions) have not given up the battles of conflict and the fight for justice. Ideas and ideals are important. Hopefully this work adds another sentence to that struggle.

*Dave Lewis*
*March 2007*

6.40   **In reaching this conclusion we have considered the primary evidence which has been put before us and the legitimate inferences which can fairly and as a matter of "common-sense and not law" be drawn from that evidence, ... .**

6.61    **I believe that the events of the last few years have not only presented British policing with a new challenge so formidable that it has come close to disaster: they have also now given the opportunity to the British Police to reinvent themselves.**

Simon Norfolk was born in Lagos, Nigeria, in 1963.
He was educated in England and gained a degree
in philosophy and sociology from Oxford and
Bristol Universities. After leaving the documentary
photography course in Newport, South Wales, he
worked for far-left publications specialising in work
on anti-racist activities and fascist groups. In 1994
he moved away from photojournalism to concentrate
on landscape photography.

Norfolk's books, *For Most Of It I Have No Words:
Genocide, Landscape, Memory* (Dewi Lewis Publishing,
Manchester, 1998) and *Afghanistan: chronotopia*
(Dewi Lewis Publishing, Manchester, 2002), have
been also exhibited at worldwide venues. Recent solo
exhibitions include *I'm sorry Dave, I'm afraid I can't
do that*, The AoP Gallery, London, 2006, and *Et in
Arcadia ego*, shown in galleries in the USA, France
and Moscow, 2006. Norfolk recently published
a book *Bleed* about the aftermath of the war in
Bosnia in 2005. He has been awarded a number of
prizes including European Publishers' Award for
Photography, 2002, The Infinity Award from the
International Centre for Photography in New York,
2004, and Le Prix Dialogue in Arles, 2005.

Norfolk now lives and works in Brighton, UK.

## Et in Arcadia ego

These photographs, divided as 'chapters', are part of the larger *Et in Arcadia ego* project attempting to understand how war and the need to fight war have formed our world, how so many of the spaces we occupy, the technologies we use and the ways we understand ourselves are created by military conflict.

The battlefields of Afghanistan and Iraq are the most obvious manifestations of this process. Conflict however can manifest itself in all manner of landscapes and surfaces created by war: from the extraordinary instant cities thrown up by refugees to the bizarre environments created by electronic eavesdropping, the cordon thrown up around US presidential hopefuls or the face of a young girl dying from AIDS in a country where an already feeble health system has been smashed by years of civil war.

What these 'landscapes' have in common, their basis in war, is fundamentally downplayed and overlooked in our society. I was astounded to discover that the long, straight, bustling, commercial road that runs through my old neighbourhood in London follows an old Roman road. In places the Roman stones are still buried beneath the modern tarmac. The road system built by the Romans was their highest military technology, their equivalent of the stealth bomber or the Apache helicopter – a technology that allowed a huge empire to be maintained by a relatively small army, that could move quickly and safely along these paved, all-weather roads. It is extraordinary that London, a city that should be shaped by Tudor kings, the British Empire, Victorian engineers and modern international finance, is a city fundamentally drawn, even to this day, by abandoned Roman military hardware.

Anybody interested in the effects of war quickly becomes an expert in ruins. These images are the result of a long fascination with ruins and their portrayal in art. Some of the earliest photographers photographed ruins. Drawing on the devastation and decay in the paintings of Nicolas Poussin and Claude Lorraine, the garden designs of Capability Brown and the poetry of Shelley and Byron, the ruins in my artworks are philosophical metaphors for the foolishness of pride, awe and the sublime, the power of God and, most importantly to me, the vanity of Empire. The photographs I am showing were all taken since 9/11, a very special time to be thinking about the making of a new global empire: the brutality necessary for its construction, and what these new ruins might mean for all of us.

*Simon Norfolk*

**Ascension Island: The Panopticon** 2003
Colour photographs
127 × 130 cm

**Ascension Island: The Panopticon**  2003
Colour photographs
127 × 130 cm

64

**Soy una raya en el mar, Mercury halide: Pa' una ciuda del norte** 2007
Colour photograph
127 × 101.6 cm

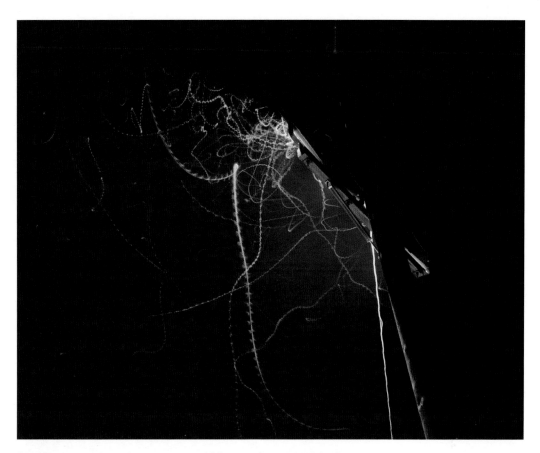

**Soy una raya en el mar, Long exposure with insects: Correr es mi destino**  2007
Colour photograph
101.6 × 127 cm

**Soy una raya en el mar, Border: De la grande Babilón**  2007
Colour photograph
101.6 × 127 cm

# T.V. Santhosh

T.V. Santhosh was born in 1968 in Kerala, India.
He initially studied painting in 1989 at the Institute
of Fine Arts in Trichur and went on to complete
a bachelor of fine arts in sculpture at Kala Bhavan
at Viswabharati University in Santiniketan, West
Bengal in 1994. Three years later, he gained a master
of fine arts in sculpture from the Faculty of Fine Arts,
Maharaja Sayajirao University of Baroda. Santhosh's
work tackles today's global issues of war and
terrorism and its representation and manipulation
by politics and the media. This paradox of reality
and manipulation is represented in the photographic
quality of his work in which identical images are
depicted in positive and negative, juxtaposed side
by side. Recent solo exhibitions include *Scars of an
Ancient Error* at the Singapore Art Fair, Singapore,
2006, and *False Promises* at the Grosvenor Gallery,
London, in collaboration with The Guild Art Gallery,
Mumbai, 2005.

Santhosh currently lives and works in Mumbai.

**Another Taxi** 2004
Oil on canvas, diptych
91.4 × 243.8 cm
Collection 'The Guild', Mumbai

## A short note

One looks at the world through the tinted spectacles of news reports that unroll the stories of massacre of innocents, spectacular highlights of explosions, flux of faces of people who make headlines, spitting the words of hate and arrogance and the kinds of propaganda campaigns that just struggle to hide nothing but truth. It is a strange world exposed and manipulated. A world where one does not know who the real enemy is, yet 'terror' is the common word for both those who resist and those who attack.

It is one's extended vision that constructs and reshapes the perceptions of the 'present'. And it is riddled with a number of eternal questions and a couple of ready-made yet elusive solutions in which I am interested. It is the touch and smell of the 'present' I am dealing with in my works, in a process to find a solution where the praxis of language becomes one with the perceptions of reality.

More recently, I have been appropriating in my works the logic of transforming a positive photographic image into its negative. Negative images evoke the inverse aspects of the phenomena. As certain elements get deleted and become unrecognisable, they reveal an event's hidden implications. In the process, the elements of 'local' lose their specificity, attaining instead a universal significance and vice versa. Marking a shift from my earlier paintings and their linguistic concerns, which dealt with a world as seen through the pages of history, which tell stories through the images of metaphors, my recent work deals with the kind of devised 'glimpses' of much larger, unresolved stories of immediate happenings.

*T.V. Santhosh*

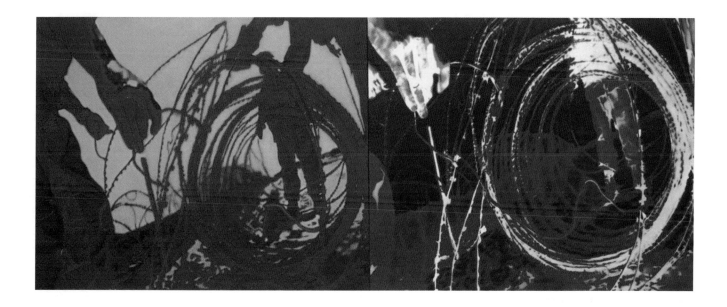

**Fear, Nation and False Promises**  2004
Oil on canvas, diptych
121.9 × 304.8 cm
Collection 'The Guild', Mumbai

**Peace Protest**  2003
Oil on canvas, diptych
119.4 × 303.5 cm
Collection of Minal and Dinesh Vazirani

# Gigi Scaria

Gigi Scaria was born in 1973 in Kothanalloor, Kerala, India. He received his bachelor of fine arts from the College of Fine Arts, Thiruvananthapuram in 1995 and a master of fine arts from Jamia Millia University, New Delhi, in 1998. Scaria's work is mainly concerned with human destiny in an urban space.

Selected exhibitions include *Where are the Amerindians?*, InterAmericas Space, CCA7 (Caribbean Contemporary Arts), Trinidad and Tobago, West Indies, 2006, and *Impossible India*, Frankfurter Kunstverein, Germany, 2006. His forthcoming projects include *Indian Photo and Media Art: A Journey of Discovery*, Vienna; *Public Places/Private Spaces: Contemporary Photography and Video Art in India*, The Newark Museum, New Jersey, USA, and *HORN PLEASE. Narratives in Contemporary Indian Art*, Switzerland.

Scaria received the 2005 Sanskrit Award for Visual Arts and was awarded the Inlaks Scholarship in 2002. He was granted the Ministry of Human Resources and Development Scholarship for Visual Arts in 1995–97 and is currently a working group member of the Khoj International Artist Association.

Scaria lives and works in New Delhi.

## A short note on my art engagements

The last 11 years of my art practice have been shaped by many factors. My studies at art school in Delhi directed my attention towards maps and mappings. When one looks at a map from a distance it imparts the effect of colourful, abstract territories. But upon close observation one comes to know that each and every abstract form and line has a place to lead and a purpose to exist within. In terms of form, structure and content, maps impart much more than the simple description of territory or geography.

As I concentrated mainly on painting and sculpture during this period, inspired by political and geographical maps, the idea of abstraction, as against specific detailing and structuring, merged into many of these works. It was a time when I treated the idea of map or mapping more as a theme to paint or sculpt without ever questioning the very formal aspect of the structure (of languages of painting, sculpture, etc.) itself.

In a later stage I tried to move away from the concept of mapping as an idea for painting. The new process demanded a great deal of mental exercise to learn the social reality using a completely different set of cartographic coordinates. The perspective of territorial mapping expanded to the mapping of culture, mapping of the environment, mapping of the hierarchies and systems of the communities we all are part of. This is where my present engagement with 'social mapping' begins.

The basic realities of the cultural, religious and ethnic identity in my immediate surroundings were a major focus at this point. As a result my reflections on social issues started to integrate into my work. The video entitled *Wounded* was my response to the communal riots and genocide that took place in Gujarat in 2002. The nine-minute video shows a man nursing his deeply wounded leg. Throughout the act of washing the wound, putting the medicine on and bandaging it, one can hear the sound of violence in the background. After bandaging he turns around and touches the tuner of a radio which is behind him. While he tries to tune the machine the viewer discovers that the sounds of crying and howling were actually coming from the radio and nowhere else. He keeps changing the stations until he finds a song. When the song starts playing he goes to sleep. This video attempts to address violence as a charged emotion that floats in the air like all other emotional elements. Maybe one has the ability to tune one's own mental position from destructive waves to a constructive one? The film hopes to indicate the fact that no remedy can cure the deeply etched mental scars of riot victims unless they make an effort to be alert/aware of the blind force of violence that they are part of.

The elements of terror and violence have come to represent the themes of dysfunction and angst for all human civilisation. All over the world citizens in all kinds of urban environments must prepare (on a daily basis) to encounter potential terror and disruption around them. My latest work, *Raise your hands those who have touched him*, tries to trace back a political murder witnessed by the city of Delhi. Mahatma Gandhi was assassinated by a fanatic on 30 January 1948. The act shocked the whole world then and led Bernard Shaw to comment 'It shows how dangerous it is to be too good'. Gandhi was killed exactly 59 years ago, a fact which reminds us that those who have met him personally or had any direct interaction with him are numbered. In another generation the memory of personal interaction with Gandhi will slip quietly from living memory. It alerts us to Albert Einstein's comment on Gandhi: 'Generations to come will scarcely believe that such a one as this ever in flesh and blood walked upon this earth.' In an attempt to record this, I attempted to find people who met Gandhi in his last days in Delhi. I would like to submit this project as a testimony, as material evidence for a trial court of the contemporary world overtaken over by historical amnesia.

With these narratives I intend to generate a multidimensional dialogue within the social system that I am a part of. Even though the boundaries are marked and specified this would be an attempt to respond and negotiate.

*Gigi Scaria*
*Delhi*

**Raise your hands those who have touched him** 2007
Five channel video on monitors and one onto the floor

# Fernando Traverso

Fernando Traverso was born in Rosario, Argentina, in 1951. He studied at the Provincial School of Visual Arts for two years but left in 1972 to become a political activist (he later finished the last two years of art school). He worked in the resistance during the military dictatorship in Argentina, during which time many of his fellow members in the resistance went missing.

Traverso's art work is centered around the imagery of bicycles, which were a common means of transport for members of the resistance – an abandoned bicycle was a sign of abduction. His work has been shown at a number of venues in his home town of Rosario and was also included in *The Disappeared* exhibition at the Museum of North Dakota, 2005, which featured Latin American artists whose work investigated the disappearance of members of the public under the dictatorships in Latin America throughout the 1970s and 1980s.

*350* speaks of the absences, of the need to fill the void left by a whole generation of enterprising young people, militants of life, anxious to change history. And they did change it, though not in the way that they had imagined. What remains of those years of violence are holes, blurred images of the 'disappeared' ones, who today gaze at us from banners carried by mothers with white scarves about their heads.

The means of transport most used by students, workers and local militants was and still is the bicycle. Many of them were left abandoned after the kidnapping and disappearance of their owners during the terrible war that followed the military coup of 24 March 1976.

I began to work with the image of an abandoned bicycle, at first putting a real bicycle at one side of an art display; then I began to screen-print them using different media, and to paint them on linen in different places.

Perhaps it was because I started to see holes in all the corners of my city that I desired to fill them. And I decided to fill them by asking a question. Because these voids are a question still unanswered for each one of us.

So it was that 350 images of abandoned bicycles began to populate the walls of Rosario, in memory of those events: one for each who had disappeared. I did the first one, I recall, in the early hours of the morning of 24 March 2001 and the last one three years later, 13 April 2004. The city became a museum of memories. Those holes began to be filled…

They are not monuments or decorations that go unnoticed in a city, as Horst Hoheisel says; these bikes make us remember at each corner, they surprise us with their presence and disturb us like enigmatic shadows. From the start, people wondered where the owner could be? Why did they abandon their bicycle here? As for the answers, we need to search for them in our memories.

Some time later the public felt the need to fill this absence, to give it a body, its own life. In this way the work of making banners was born. People brought pieces of fabric which would be filled with the silhouettes of the ownerless bicycles. This image will no longer exist alone, somebody has taken it further, to open doors inside other stories. Many of these banners, every so often, are seen on the streets in various demonstrations: on the 24 March, to mark some activist declaration or simply as a banner at a music festival.

This collaborative project culminates on the web through images that people send from different parts of the world, showing the destiny of the banners which were made in one of the many projects that I have carried out in different cities, so weaving a compact web of 'memories' which takes visual form on the website www.fernandotraverso.com.

Given that this symbol has become part of the collective, I will incorporate a manual on how to make a stencil of the bicycle onto the web, so that whoever wants to make one can do so without difficulty. In this very way several groups of young people in various parts of the world are making them, taking the proposal into the cities and speaking of each one of their forgotten ones.

*Fernando Traverso*
*Translated by Melanie Vial*

**350, Intervención urbana, Rosario** 2001–04
Colour photographs
30.5 × 40.6 cm

**350, Intervención urbana, Rosario**  2001–04
Colour photographs
30.5 × 40.6 cm

# Between Yes and No

'Let your communication be, Yea, yea; Nay, nay:
for whatsoever is more than these cometh of evil.'
Jesus of Nazareth (Matthew 5:37)

In 1947, the year India gained independence and Pakistan was created, six painters based in Bombay aligned themselves to a style European in origin and internationalist in outlook. They called themselves the Progressive Artists' Group and became 'the most "correctly" modernist'[1] among many similar associations then springing up in Indian cities. The nature of modernism as it developed in India, however, was very different from its trajectory in the place of its birth. European modernism matured during the belle époque, a period of peace within the continent and massive imperialist expansion without. The Edwardian idyll of the early 20th century was, of course, merely the calm before a dreadful storm. Artists who recognised this fact heralded the coming age of extremes[2] by creating an art of extremes. Picasso's *Les Demoiselles D'Avignon*, painted exactly a 100 years ago, perfectly represents the extremist spirit of European modernism: it is brutal, sensationalist, uncompromising, courageous.

This approach was adopted by a lone painter in India, Francis Newton Souza (1924–2002), ideologue of the Progressive Artist's Group. It is the work of Souza's comrade M F Husain (1915–), however, which appears with hindsight to be characteristic of Indian modernism. It rejected the programmatic dehumanisation of its European progenitor, a dehumanisation valorised not only by critics on the far right like T E Hulme, and on the far left like Clement Greenberg, but also by liberals such as Ortega y Gasset. For mid-20th century Indians, living in the aftermath of two unimaginably destructive world wars and, closer to home, a famine which took millions of lives followed by internecine violence which claimed a million more, extremism appeared the last thing art should celebrate. The alternative offered by Gandhi and Nehru, of building on India's syncretic tradition to create an inclusive, independent nation, seemed far more appealing. Gandhi and Nehru had impeccable anti-imperialist credentials, but were also deified in independent India. They were simultaneously revolutionary heroes and establishment icons. An adherence to their vision complicated the categories of rebellion and conformism.

No matter how critical artists grew of particular deficiencies in the state's functioning, there was, somewhere within their work, a celebration of the idea of India. No matter how gruesome the subjects they chose, their treatment held out at least a faint hope of the possibility of healing. In each case where the influence of a European movement was felt, it was modified by humanist impulses. Painters borrowed from cubism, but never represented man and mandolin without distinction in the manner of Braque. They tried their hand at abstraction, but did not, as Malevich had done, produce geometric images informed by machines with no echoes of life forms or landscapes. They did not desire to condemn the past wholesale as the futurists had done in Italy. India's culture had, after all, already been denigrated by imperialists like Thomas Macaulay who, in his *Minute on Education* of 1835, argued for 'the intrinsic superiority of the Western literature' and asserted that 'a single shelf of a good European library' was 'worth the whole native literature of India and Arabia'.

Of the major early 20th-century art movements, it was expressionism that found most favour within the subcontinent, but, as handled by Satish Gujral (1925–) and Chittaprosad Bhattacharya (1915–78), who depicted horrors experienced before and during partition in the Punjab and Bengal respectively, the ruthless angularity of *Die Brücke* was softened to the point of sentimentality. Melodrama, anathema to the modernist aesthetic but a central and enduring feature of India's narrative tradition, seeped into post-independence painting. Though it was allowed in with the best intentions, it turned art soggy with emotion.

By the 1960s, the nation's experiment with new forms had found only partial success. The choice appeared to be between transparent derivativeness on the one hand, and backsliding into emotionally appealing romanticism on the other. The way out of this impasse involved a long detour into semi-abstraction, into a search for the occult and the numinous in local traditions.

By the end of the 1960s, ripples of revolutionary impulses reached Indian shores. Maoist intellectuals attempted to kick start a peasants' movement with the aim of transforming the Indian state. In 1975, prime minister Indira Gandhi, claiming the nation was sliding toward anarchy, declared an emergency, suspending civil rights and clamping down on press freedom. It lasted 18 months, before she revoked her order and declared fresh elections, which brought the first non-Congress government to power.

In this highly charged decade, painters reconnected with public issues and found robust forms to express their political concerns. The new figuration of the 1970s was manifestly contemporary without being derivative, drawing confidently both on the Euro-American tradition and an eclectic range of indigenous sources. It carried an emotive charge without ever turning maudlin. Bhupen Khakhar (1934–2003), Gulammohammed Sheikh (1937–), Arpita Singh (1937–), Jogen Chowdhury (1939–) and Sudhir Patwardhan (1949–) were the crucial artists in this breakthrough phase. The list is a personal one: most critics would give equal prominence to Vivan Sundaram (1943–), Nilima Sheikh (1945–), Nalini Malani (1946–) and Gieve Patel (1946–).

The bedrock of art, film and theatre in the 1970s was Marxism. Whether committed to a Marxist India or liberals with a respect for the writings of Marx and his followers, artists gravitated to the notion that their output, in order to be relevant, had to be an agent for social and political change. Yet they produced little that was aggressive or determined to shock. When, in the late 1970s, Bhupen Khakhar began to create paintings related to his homosexuality, it wasn't in an activist temper. His images were quirky, sometimes downright funny, frequently melancholy, and always impossible to analyse into a clear message. If the decade of the strongest political commitment did not produce confrontationist art, it's not surprising that the trend continued into the postmodern era with its privileging of irony, play and surface.

It is worth asking why Indians generally have shied away from creating work that is 'in-your-face'. Certainly, the complicated history of colonialism has played a role, but there are at least three other major factors. The first is the exceptional directness and moralising in popular representation. This is as much a feature of Bollywood extravaganzas as it is of the traditional Ramlila in which the story of the Ramayana is staged. Actors take a stance and declaim. Ambiguity of any sort is frowned upon. Every action must be driven by a clear intention, and the difference between what is virtuous and what condemnable communicated through exaggerated expressions and gestures. Artists react against this by choosing ambiguity, subtlety and indirection. It isn't only a case of *AfterShock*, but also of *AfterSchlock*.

The second issue concerns the use of language. As demonstrated by Okwui Enwezor's text-laden Documenta 11, political art today is immersed in language. In India this immediately leads to the question: which language? The answer among artists is usually 'English' because that greatly enhances the chance of being noticed by international curators. But, English is spoken well only by an elite, far smaller in size than many would like to believe. Images are more democratic than written words. They have existed for at least a 100,000 years, created by people from all strata of society. Writing has been around for less than one-tenth of that time and has been, for much of that period, the domain of a powerful minority. In India images were the province of the lower castes, writing the monopoly of the highest. There can be no counterparts of *Act Up* in India, nor of the *Guerrilla Girls*, because the use of text for egalitarian ends, within the context of global visual arts practice, risks being bogged down in insurmountable contradictions.

The last and most pernicious influence on the nature of art is censorship. Not only are there stringent laws governing art production and display, but these are backed by popular support. The vast majority of people believe that, in a country fraught with conflict, where a riot between groups appears always round the corner, amity must be protected even if it means suppressing everything which could outrage sensitivities. Self-censorship becomes a part of every Indian artist's frame of mind.

There has been, over the past few years, a worrying rise in proscription by the mob. As I write this, a student of the best fine arts faculty in the country at the M S University in Baroda (Vadodara) has been taken into custody for exhibiting images allegedly offensive to Hindus and Christians. A group of activists from the Vishwa Hindu Parishad (VHP), assisted by policemen, barged into the university grounds during the annual display, vandalised artworks and roughed up the student, named Chandramohan. The police arrested him and refused to countenance any complaints against the violent activists. It is no coincidence that the act took place in Gujarat, a state ruled by the right-wing Hindu Bharatiya Janata Party (BJP) where a horrific anti-Muslim pogrom was carried out in 2002 with the collusion of politicians, bureaucrats and policemen.

Similar disruptions, however, could break out anywhere in the country and target anybody, even the 91-year-old M F Husain, India's most famous painter and the recipient of some of the highest state honours. Husain is a Muslim who celebrates Hindu iconography, but his reinterpretations have raised the hackles of the Hindu right. He has been hounded for nearly a decade, his paintings defaced in places as far away as London, and cases filed against him in courts across India, forcing him into quasi-exile in Dubai.

Such hypersensitivity about representation is linked to the rise of identity politics since the 1980s. That decade saw the inauguration of secessionist insurgencies by Sikhs in Punjab and Muslims in Jammu and Kashmir. Hindu parties used these to argue that secularism had failed, and a hardline approach was needed to secure the nation's unity and the rights of the majority. Their initial campaign targeted a mosque in the town of Ayodhya, supposedly built on the site of a demolished temple at a spot which the faithful consider Lord Rama's birthplace. The 460-year-old mosque itself was razed in 1992 and, within five years, India's first government led by a non-secular party was in power at the centre.

At around the same time that religious conflict was gaining momentum, the Indian economy was loosening the shackles of the so-called license raj, which had severely restricted private investment and discouraged multinational companies. The process of liberalisation began in earnest in 1991, just when the agitation to replace the Babri mosque with a temple was at its peak. The phenomena of globalisation and sectarianism soon became the twin foci of avowedly political art in India.

On 11 September, 2001, the centre of the globalised financial world was impacted devastatingly by the politics of religious identity. Those such as Damien Hirst, engaged within the tradition of an art of extremes, saw how the attack related to their own work. He said of it, 'Of course, it's visually stunning and you've got to hand it to them on some level because they've achieved something which nobody would have ever have thought possible – especially to a country as big as America. So on one level they kind of need congratulating.'[3] Compare this response with Atul Dodiya's take on Mahatma

Gandhi: 'I came across a quote from Gandhi where he said, "I am an artist of non-violence", not a philosopher of non-violence. That led me to see that in all his acts, his wearing of khadi, the Dandi march to make salt, the structure of his ashram, he was like a conceptual and performance artist'.[4] If Gandhi was the greatest artist of non-violence in the 20th century, Bin Laden has become the foremost artist of violence in the 21st.

The question is whether the art of shock can respond adequately to 9/11, the events consequent to it, and the revolution in technology which has paralleled them. At the click of a mouse now we can access the most horrific and most intimate moments in the lives of hundreds of individuals. Here is Saddam Hussein hanging from a noose, neck broken. Here's a Yezidi girl being bludgeoned to death for loving a Sunni Arab man. Here's a boy beheading a hostage without a hint of the revulsion one sees on the face of Caravaggio's David. Can art get more visceral than these amateur videos, or more spectacular than the collapsing towers? Or are we at the end of the art of extremes, and irrevocably in the age of AfterShock?

*Girish Shahane is a freelance writer based in Bombay (Mumbai). He has written and lectured extensively about Indian contemporary art for the past 12 years. He was editor and later consulting editor of the Art News Magazine of India. He currently contributes a column to the Bombay edition of Time Out magazine.*

1. Geeta Kapur. *When Was Modernism: Essays on Contemporary Cultural Practice in India*, Tulika, New Delhi, 2000, p. 304.
2. A phrase chosen by Hobsbawn to characterise his history of the short 20th century. Eric Hobsbawn, *The Age of Extremes: A History of the World 1914–1991*, Vintage, New York, 1996.
3. Hirst's interview with the BBC can be seen at: http://news.bbc.co.uk/1/hi/in_depth/world/2002/september_11_one_year_on/2229628.stm
4. Quoted in 'The Dodiya Style' by Girish Shahane, *Man's World* magazine, June 2003.

# Why Do These People Hate Us? The Legacy of Colonialism.

In the weeks that followed the terrible events of 11 September, 2001, the question 'Why do these people hate us?' was a constant refrain in the news reports from New York. Beyond the collective sense of shock and astonishment at the startling, terrifying violence that had sealed the twin towers' fate, there was also a sense that these events were entirely unexpected. Yet, if war is the logical (if unfortunate) consequence of the extension of foreign policy when diplomatic means have failed, then perhaps we should also acknowledge the role that military adventurism plays as a recruiting sergeant to the ranks of violent fundamentalism.

A study of the foreign policies of the great powers in the 20th century is a history of first the European powers (France, Germany and Great Britain) and, after the second world war, the United States and the Soviet Union extending their spheres of influence into the developing world. Whether the empires thereby created are either formal (the British Empire) or (supposedly) informal (Anglo-American entanglement in Iraq), and whether imperial policies are applied directly by governments or by commercial agencies acting on their behalf (the British East India Company in India and Halliburton in Iraq), their purpose, almost exclusively, is to secure control over the world's resources – spices, silks and cotton in the 18th and 19th centuries, oil in the 21st.

Throughout history, an increasingly sophisticated rationale, expressed in phrases like 'civilising mission', has been employed to justify the divide-and-rule tactics of colonialism, a historical progression whose core themes can be reduced to racism, avarice and to a lesser extent geo-strategic advantage. A fascinating and deeply disturbing development of neo-colonialism in the 21st century has been the use of propaganda to create the climate of consent required to justify offensive action, most recently against Iraq in the court of (principally) American public opinion. In *Conversations on the Post 9/11 World*, Noam Chomsky suggests that in the modern United States, an effective strategy for driving a domestic agenda based on tax cuts for the rich, the decimation of social security benefits, reduced protection for working people and the maintenance of the wealth and influence of elites, is to keep the general population in a state of fear. If people believe their security is threatened they will gravitate toward a strong leader who is perceived to protect them from enemies real or imagined. An important part of this agenda is the temporary suppression of peoples' domestic concerns as a by-product of the 'state of emergency' in which they find themselves. Prior to the current conflict in Iraq, George Bush was presented in the US media as a resolute wartime leader – indeed the only leader – with the necessary determination to overcome an 'awesome foe' (Iraq), an enemy chosen precisely because it was practically defenceless and could be crushed in no time.[1]

The phrase 'regime change' is a recent addition to the lexicon of colonialism and entered the wider public consciousness during the run-up to the Iraq war. The desire, expressed openly and without embarrassment, to 'change a regime' neatly describes the uncomfortable realisation that third-world countries have the capability to wield what, to western eyes, are unacceptable levels of influence over their own natural resources.[2] The historical precedents for regime change, which have been played out so tragically in 21st-century Iraq, are well documented and were, in the first instance, a by-product of British colonial expansion between the wars. The British, when they supplanted the Ottoman Turks as the colonial masters of Iraq in the 1920s, led the way in developing the principle of ruling through facades. It was the British who first pioneered the use of despotic native rulers who, in places like Iraq, were allowed build up vast fortunes and impregnable power by exploiting ethnic tensions and internecine strife,[3] simultaneously enjoying the protection and masking the location of 'real' power.

As empires have unravelled, from the disintegration of the Soviet Union to the death of Yugoslavia, violent enmities have been unleashed between ethnic communities, which had lived peacefully side by side, before being freed from unifying opposition to the imperialist yoke. Even when the true identity of the colonial master is undisguised as it was in British India, the motivation to divide-and-rule seems to have been a prerequisite to the maintenance of colonial power. In India the departure of the British led to the displacement of the burden of imperialism and an allocation of resources, a distribution of income and the responsibilities of statehood skewed in favour of one strata of society or ethnic community at the expense of others. Given that the British Raj had nourished Muslim separatism as a foil to the nationalism of the Congress party,[4] there seems an inevitability about the partition of India, the fearsome communal riots that attended it, and the factor that relationships between Hindus and Muslims continue to play within India and in relations between India and Pakistan.

The history of Bengal, the site of the first encroachment of the British East India company into the subcontinent nearly 400 years ago, however, suggests that divide-and-rule is not the only possible outcome for a multi-faith, multi-ethnic society, even one under colonial domination. The recent British Museum exhibition *Myths of Bengal* offered a tantalising glimpse of syncretism – exchange and commonality across cultures – where Hindus and Muslims shared sites of pilgrimage and Bauls, itinerant troubadours from both faiths, used the same songs to share with a largely illiterate population their yearnings for god. These songs were a great inspiration to the Bengali poet Rabinbanrath Tagore (a Hindu), whose poems were adopted as national anthems by both predominantly Muslim Bangladesh (in 1971) and predominantly Hindu India (in 1947).[5]

In a fascinating article in the the Guardian in November 2006, Madeleine Bunting described Bengal as one of the world's great melting pots and the place where 'perhaps East has met West for the longest period of settled co-existence'. She also recognised Bengal's painful and difficult history since the partition of India in 1947 and suggested that perhaps one of the reasons why Bengali syncretism hasn't survived, is repeated attempts to 'purify' Bengali culture directed by reform movements within both Islam and Hinduism. These were (sadly) carried forward as people of both faiths became increasingly literate and educated, aided and abetted (almost inevitably) by a clumsy British colonial policy.

From Northern Ireland to India, the attempts of the British Empire to control its overseas possessions resulted in the exacerbation of ethnic tensions and, from the moment that Britain began to divest itself of its colonial possessions, independence settlements that redefined the identity of entire regions in terms of a single faith community. Succumbing to partition in 1947, a common culture and language proved unable to hold Bengal together, and yet neither was a common religious identity able to hold Pakistan together in the form in which it emerged from the Empire. Bangladesh, formerly East Pakistan, fought Pakistan for its independence in 1971.[6]

In their concentration on the lives and experiences of individuals wrestling with legacies of unravelling empires, and the military, political and economic neo-colonialism of the early 21st century, artists like Shilpa Gupta, Simon Norfolk and Alfredo Jaar ask searching questions of western audiences and question the historical patterns of imperial domination, perhaps providing the beginnings of an understanding of the violent animus which lies at the heart of violent fundamentalism. If we recognise the historical progression of colonialism and neo-colonialism, we must also recognise the repeating pattern in which oppressed or subject peoples respond to colonial domination and the unravelling of empires. This can also manifest itself in the form of non-violence as practised by Mahatma Gandhi. In the modern world, however, it seems more likely to take the form of the unspeakable violence we have seen tragically played out on the streets of Dar-es-Salaam, Madrid, London and New York over the last 10 years. If we are truly to address the root causes of these conflicts we should perhaps be asking not 'why do these people hate us?', but, 'why is our understanding of these peoples' hatred for us so limited?'. The portents of current global conflict have, after all, been inscribed in history for many generations. In December 2002 the Monthly Review, an American news magazine, used a quote from a 1919 essay on ancient Rome, entitled the 'Sociology of Imperialisms', by Austrian economist Josef Schumpeter as a comparison with George Bush's national security strategy:

'There was no corner of the world where some interest was not alleged to be in danger or under actual attack. If the interests were not Roman, they were of Rome's allies: and if Rome had no allies, then allies would be invented. When it was utterly impossible – why then it was the national honour that had been insulted. The fight was always invested with an aura of legality. Rome was always being attacked by evil-minded neighbours, always fighting for breathing space. The whole world was pervaded by enemies, and it was manifestly Rome's duty to guard against their indubitably aggressive designs.'[7]

In an equally disturbing augury of the shape of things to come, British observers noted that the horrendous casualties suffered by Sudanese dervishes at the battle of Omdurman outside Khartoum in 1898 (13,000 against 48 for the British army) was the result not only of the British army's technological superiority, but, tellingly, a commitment to Islam which made the dervishes indifferent to death.[8] The 2003 invasion of Iraq would suggest that, in spite of ample historical precedents, western capitalism seems unwilling to acknowledge either the resentment that its imperial adventures have caused, or understand that the fearsome violence unleashed on the twin towers or the London underground may be a consequence of these adventures.

In an age increasingly polarised by the inequities of global capitalism and the supposedly mutually exclusive religious identities and ethnic tensions that have grown from it, the history of Bengal exposes the falseness of the 'clash of civilisations' thesis propounded by American social scientist Samuel Huntingdon.[9]

Sadly, we must conclude that the past offers more enlightened models of living with difference than have been achieved in the modern world. As the history of Bengal teaches us, some of the world's richest cultural traditions are the legacy of tolerance, understanding and the interaction of several faiths and cultural traditions. As Madeleine Bunting put it in the Guardian in November 2006: 'We need to be reminded – and inspired – by the history of places such as Bengal, so that we may guard against the parcelling of human beings into discrete civilisational categories based on faith'[10].

A greater mutual respect between different faiths, economic and cultural traditions might also go some way toward neutering the violent animus that has been directed against the West since the early 1990s.

*Matthew Shaul is head of programming and operations at the University of Hertfordshire Galleries. A specialist in contemporary art from the former East Germany, most recently curated the touring exhibition 'Do Not Refreeze – Photography Behind the Berlin Wall'.*

1. Noam Chomsky, *Imperial Ambitions – Conversations on the Post 9/11 World, Interviews with David Barsamian*, Metropolitan Books, New York, 2005, p. 25.
2. Karl De Schweinitz (Jr), *The Rise and Fall of British India*, Methuen, London, 1983, p. 253.
3. Noam Chomsky, ibid., pp. 45–48.
4. B.N. Pandey, *The Break-up of British India*, London, Macmillan, 1969, p. 215.
5. Madeleine Bunting, 'A Tradition Which Ridicules the Clash of Civilisations', *the Guardian*, 29/11/2006 (The assertion (by implication) in Madeleine Bunting's article is that Tagore's poems had been originally written as (rather than posthumously adopted as) the national anthems of the two countries: an impossibility given that Tagore died in 1941 prior to Indian independence in 1947 and the creation of, first East Pakistan, and then, in 1971, Bangladesh).
6. Madeleine Bunting, ibid.
7. Josef Schumpeter quoted in Noam Chomsky, ibid., p. 53.
8. Karl De Schweinitz (Jr), ibid., pp. 241–242.
9. & 10. Madeleine Bunting, ibid.

# Radical Uncertainty and Elegiac Practices

'Representation follows two laws: it always conveys more than it intends; and it is never totalising. The "excess" meaning conveyed by representation creates a supplement that makes multiple and resistant readings possible.'[1]

*AfterShock*: the title suggests a remainder; excess that comes after the event, unsettling the usual order. It suggests drawing in some new awareness – after the event. The spectacles of 9/11 and Abu Ghraib are pressing reminders of the battles being fought through representation. We live in a time and place, in the West, where the rhetorics of otherness fuse uncomfortably with the rhetoric of the threat of Muslim fundamentalist bombs. The popular press often have invoked the language of Orientalism, 'othering' those who have lived many years and been educated in the West.[2] The politicians who peddle the neo-liberal dream do so by offering the certainty of being right and deliverance through war.[3] Certainty relies on a simple vision of the world, therefore positing complexity and heterogeneity may cultivate a resistance to the presently popular impulse for fashioning conflict and nurturing it into easy redemptions.[4] What is at stake for this exhibition, to be shown in England at this time? Uncertainty is what art can offer, a radical uncertainty that resists persuasive narratives: to incur any disruption, therefore to the certainty that is offered as a staple in the West, could be seen as a promise of hope, a prerequisite of change.

There are many ways to resist: one may wish to reflect on the fashions of conflict through the negative dialectic of wars that do not currently inhabit the news. The work of David Farrell or Ian Charlesworth that reflects on the continuing residues of the uneasy peace in Northern Ireland invites us in turn to reflect on what we are to make of the Troubles in Ireland now there are no longer IRA bombs in London. In this context I am invited to compare the threats on Britain's recent past, with the current prolonged hysteria around possible threats of 'Muslim bombs' imagined as more out of control and more evil in the popular press than the bombs we had before, even though at the time, in the 1980s the IRA were imagined as terrorists also.[5] Forgetting that these kinds of shifts are made allows us to just surrender to the moment, giving rise to a circus of posturing from overly conscientious airport security guards, absurdly irrelevant citizenship tests for those wishing to become British citizens and from the ever increasing language of border control that focuses on the 'good' and 'bad' object as minority 'other' in Europe. Although I write this in the aftermath of local elections where the British National Party has not made the inroads it hoped for at this time of xenophobic rhetoric, it is nonetheless a dangerous turn that pits more people against each other in a hierarchy of otherness from the 'model minority' downwards. The LA riots in 1992 taught us that even the 'model minority' (who in this case were the Korean immigrants), who separate themselves from those less desirable, less invisible others, could only rely on their own

resources while the state protects the privilege of a certain class of whiteness[6].

The brinkmanship between India and Pakistan has been in the limelight since the attacks on the world trade centre in the US. The work of artists such as Amar Kanwar, Atul Dodiya and T.V. Santhosh consciously reverberates from within this contemporary setting. While not referring directly to the tragedy of partitioning in 1947 on the Indian subcontinent, the past sits underneath the current situation and is a shadow to the work, arguably allowing the viewer to reflect on the continuing aftermath of other partitions across religious or ethnic lines that produced and keep producing their own, seemingly irresolvable, aftershocks.

In looking at these conflicts in their complex artistic articulation of excess, can it help to make different decisions, work towards other solutions than to those currently presented to us through the current singular narrative of Islam, Iraq and the West? Brought together in this way, the work in the exhibition posits a complex world that represents many difficult historical and geographical moments, not often discussed in the media, such as South America, or Rwanda, as well as Ireland and India/Pakistan, already mentioned. Contemplating such possibilities is the promise of this exhibition that resists through a heterogeneous approach to the world's struggles for power.

If heterogeneity offers enough complexity for a radical uncertainty then we must by the same token, be wary of equivalences. What does this mean within the British context? After all, the work of these artists is showing within a British institution and will therefore be read through those cultural contexts. One impact of 9/11 in New York and its sister bombings of Madrid, March 2004, or 7/7 in London has been the considerable shift in debates around minority groups. While in the mid 1990s, Tariq Modood was doing important but relatively unheeded work writing that the anti-racist accounts were preoccupied with colour racism and thereby ignoring the centrality of culture and religion in the formation of subjectivity through faith, race and geographic specificity. Now in a manoeuvre that represents a complete *volte-face*, faith has become the new race.[7] The turn to redefine otherness in relation to faith (or what could be called a faith turn) not only obscures the complexities of identity formation but also places a false emphasis on what constitutes a so-called 'faith' community. Faith has come to mean Muslim (and to a lesser extent Jew or Sikh) and Muslims have been racialised into a fixed category – which sets up a false hierarchy of motivational forces – only Muslims are guided so completely (read: dangerously) by their faith: Christians, particularly in England, are imagined as so rational and reasonable according to this prejudicial logic. That logic fails to take into account that Christianity can be equally strange and irrational to those not formed through it: Christianity is, of course, naturalised in a country such as Britain, which does not make a distinction between church and state. It also fails to take into account that many who may be identified as Muslims (or Jews or Sikhs) actually live secular lives. Indeed, many Christians are guided primarily by the teachings of Christianity (or their Christian faith) and at times in opposition to state law, anti-abortion lobbies being an obvious case in point.[8] To name a group a 'faith group' makes it the defining feature and serves to force choices into religion where none need be. There has been a turn to faith in many communities, not just in those whose origin is Muslim: the politics of the Middle East has felt the impact of a certain kind of support from fundamentalist Christians in the United States, for example through its foreign policy as well as independent aid from those communities. Furthermore, that not every Muslim is a fundamentalist, nor even practising is a testimony to the flaw in the term: faith cannot therefore be the principal factor of adherence to community and it is dangerous to make it so. Is it, primarily faith that defines a Muslim, Jew or Sikh?[9] Is it a combination of many things – community, antecedents, life lived, action, not altogether unlike Stuart Hall's definition of ethnicity as an articulation in process or perhaps Paul Gilroy's anti-anti-essentialism, where he states that black identity is constituted through a lived experience that 'remains the outcome of practical activity: language, gesture, bodily significations, desires.'[10]

The underlying discussions on faith groups are thus part of the same continuum of race speech with a superficial gloss on faith in the contemporary turn. The inclusion, therefore, of *Chapter Six – Racism* in an exhibition like this by Dave Lewis crucially serves, to remind us not only of how recent the rise in the 'Islamic question' is in the debates on 'otherness' but that it has, as a media debate, virtually elided the experiences and the conditions that created the MacPherson report: conditions that remain unresolved and recommendations that are yet to be addressed.[11]

If there is a return[12] to faith it arises in Britain partly out of ambiguous demands on those from so called 'faith groups' to adhere, on the one hand to 'British values' that make claims to secularisation, while underlying British rhetoric on the other hand adheres, in its 'white flight' to some lingering foundational myths of homogeneity and ruralism that interweaves class into the mix. In this context it is important to remember an earlier moment highlighted by Ian Chambers. In the text *Unrealized Democracy and a Posthumanist Art* (2003)[13] Chambers discusses the importance of interrupting the postcolonial through the ability of art to resite and recite. He gives the example of the film by Gurinder Chadha, *I'm British But…* (1990). In this film a group of young Asian musicians play Bhangra music on a rooftop in Southall. This re-treading of the image of the Beatles playing *Get Back* on top of the Apple studios is not a copy, argues Chambers, but an instance of re-emergence out of the same (or rather similar) context, geographically, historically, an 'articulation of difference springing up in the same place' but also 'a particular and local urban elaboration, springing out of the same complex locality as the earlier metropolitan Britain represented by the Beatles'[14] that could only exist through a celebration of emerging out of two homes: Asia *and* Britain.

But what of art? How does it translate in the global cultural exchange?[15] A radical contribution of this exhibition is that it does not draw from one artistic strategy. Although taking from documentary imagery, some of the artists, such as Atul Dodiya, Alfredo Jaar or Jitish Kallat, translate this into art through more traditional forms, eschewing the prevailing Atlantacist orthodoxy of photographic imagery as *in itself* a radical, problematising format. Furthermore, these are translations that derive from different ends of the art world hierarchy, contesting fashions in artistic strategies as well as geographical hot spots[16].

Nonetheless, some histories of documentary photography are constitutive in the case of this exhibition. Julian Stallabrass[17] has argued that the spectacle is avoided in documentary practices today and that it represents a post-humanist moment in photographic practices that is far from the utopian decisive moment of Bresson or of the politics of the everyday. This impulse can be seen in much contemporary art. The figure is absent – there is no longer a belief in human agency and the suffering human is no longer a motivator towards revolution. In part it derives from the influence of photographers like Richard Misrach who documented the bombed and polluted Nevada desert and the censorship in the US of Vietnam photographers such as Phillip Jones Griffiths. The trope forces the viewer to slow down – to avoid the interpellative call of the policeman to 'move along, there is nothing to see'.[18] This aim can be seen in the work of Simon Norfolk (one of Stallabrass' examples), who photographs with a large-format camera the place where battle scenes *have taken place* and also in the work of Fernando Traverso, who has spray-painted the impression of bicycles, in the streets of Rosario, Argentina, and photographed the results to signify the absence of persons disappeared in the 'Dirty War' and of course in David Farrell's work. These artists are working with representation as absence, as anti-spectacle or, in the language of Phelan, as unmarked. However, according to Stallabrass, it is merely that there is no impetus to shock: the audience is assumed to need more subtle promptings in a gallery setting. Stallabrass asks whether the gallery is the right place for revolutionary practices: elegiac emptiness is now a conventional trope that merely speaks to yet another aesthetic rather than challenging the status quo, especially within a context of managed capitalism (and managed difference).

But maybe Stallabras is asking too much of art. Peggy Phelan in *Unmarked: The Politics of Performance* questions the relationship between representational visibility and political power and suggests that the radical possibility and contribution of art is that it is never totalising. If resolution is to be sought out in life, is it indeed to be sought out in art? Resolution implies the end of struggle and conflict. Or should we strive to look for what does not add up, the punctum that disrupts the story, the subject that displaces what we thought was the subject? Or to put it in the terms of Chambers, 'The Art of interruption, art as interruption, both brings to light our prescribed state – its limits and location in time and place – while also opening out on to the possibility of revisiting, reciting (in the sense of reworking), and resiting (in the sense of transporting) those languages elsewhere'.[19]

*AfterShock* brings together work that resites and recites – the breadth and scope of artistic strategies in this exhibition articulates subtle interfaces between the political, the aesthetic and the social. The exhibition does the crucial work of highlighting complex viewpoints, shifting valencies and the interdependencies of power relations as they play out through history, around the world. In such mediated societies as those of the western world, mounting an exhibition that suggests different problematics around war on this scale to the prevalent narrative is an important opportunity to think beyond the parameters that we have been given to understand the mistakes of the war in Iraq and the place of Britain within it. Furthermore, it gives us the opportunity to understand the crucial place that global power relations play in the awareness of the West of conflict: that faith or the 'clash of civilizations' are subordinate to post-colonial legacies and constitutive of a Manichean colonial mindset that still prevails.

*Dr Rachel Garfield is an artist and writer currently teaching visual arts at the University of Salford.*

Many thanks to John Timberlake, for his ongoing love, support and insights.

1. Peggy Phelan, *Unmarked: The Politics of Performance*, Routledge, 1993, p. 2.
2. Orientalism, as framed by Edward Said. Please also see Paul Gilroy, *After Empire: Melancholia or Convivial Culture?*, Routledge, 2004, pp. 137–144. that reflects on the popular discussions and perceptions of Richard Reid and Zacarias Moussaoui.
3. Tony Blair is a case in point here.
4. It is now widely accepted that the invasion of Iraq was based on flawed arguments of links with Bin Laden and of the capabilities of Iraq to destroy the West with weapons that still haven't been found. The language of the invasion 'clash of civilisations'; 'shock and awe' have a religious redemptive message.
5. I am talking specifically about the media hysteria in the aftermath of 9/11; the invasion of two sovereign countries; of the way that information is released on ever more spectacular failed plots like the one last summer in Britain involving numerous airplanes colliding in the sky and the panic that ensues such as the grinding to a halt of the airports last summer in Britain: this kind of hysteria was not present during the IRA bombing campaigns. See also footnote 2.
6. See Sumi K. Cho, 'Korean Americans vs. African Americans: Conflict and Construction' in *Reading Rodney King: Reading Urban Uprising*, Robert Gooding-Williams (ed.), Routledge, 1993, pp. 196–301. The 'model minority' is assigned the role of minority group able to integrate into the middle class. We might also usefully be reminded here of the history of the Irish as 'other' in Britain.
7. 'Faith group' is a now a funding category in the management of difference.
8. Notably, Tony Blair on many occasions claimed to have followed his conscience into war with Iraq as his defence to the people of Britain although this could be seen as an appeal to moderate Muslims.
9. This is especially cogent in religions that are based in ritual.
10. Gilroy, ibid., p. 102.
11. Ibid., p. 144, Gilroy discusses directly the link between the MacPherson report and the attraction of some young black British men towards fundamentalist Islam.
12. I use this word with reticence as it implies a naturalisation of a process that I don't mean to emphasise.
13. Ian Chambers, 'Unrealized Democracy and a Posthumanist Art', *Democracy Unrealized: Documenta 11_Platform1*, Okwui Enwezor, Carlos Basualdo, Ute Meta Bauer, et al., Hatje Cantz, 2002, pp. 169–178.
14. Ibid., p. 174.
15. Miwon Kwon has famously suggested that the site of work is now the discursive field in which it operates. She suggests that work can travel around the global biennales because of a universal language of art that defies the specificity of place and time and arises out of a neominimalist hegemony that stands in for difference.
16. Documenta XI aimed to have a global reach, however the exhibition demonstrated the effects of the power of the commercial art sector that gave considerable prominence to some artists in the manner of display. See PhD, Rachel Garfield, *Identity Politics and Performativity; Encounters with Recent Jewish Art* (unpublished 2003).
17. This has been taken from a conference paper delivered at the V&A, entitled *Siting the Photograph: Between Wall Page and Screen*, 10 May 2003. Although this is a history of western documentary, I would argue the point of Miwon Kwon, who suggests that work can travel around the global biennales because of a universal language of art that defies the specificity of place and time and arises out of a neominimalist hegemony that stands in for difference.
18. Jacques Ranciere as quoted in Nicholas Mirzeoff, *Watching Babylon: The War in Iraq and Global Visual Culture*, Routledge, 2005, p. 16.
19. Ibid., pp. 173–174.

# List of works

**The Atlas Group/Walid Raad**

**We Can Make Rain But No One Came To Ask**  2005
Single-channel video projection with sound, 17 mins
Courtesy Anthony Reynolds Gallery, London

**François Bucher***

**White Balance (to think is to forget differences)**  2002
Single-channel video projection with sound, 32 mins

**Ian Charlesworth***

**From Dark Passages**  2007
Carbon, resin and gesso on board
400 × 500 cm

**Atul Dodiya**

**Page from a Diary**  1998
Watercolour on paper
55.9 × 76.2 cm
Courtesy of Sangita Jindal, Mumbai

**Sale of Khadi**  1998
Watercolour on paper
178 × 115 cm
Collection Galerie Mirchandani + Steinruecke,
Mumbai

**The Route to Dandi**  1998
Watercolour, marble dust and charcoal
pencil on paper
172.7 × 111.7 cm
Private collection

**Juan Manuel Echavarría**

**Bocas de Ceniza/Mouths of Ash**  2003–04
Single channel digital video with sound,
18 mins

**David Farrell***

**Innocent Landscapes, Oristown**  2000
Colour photograph
55 × 55 cm

**Innocent Landscapes, Oristown**  1999
Colour photograph
55 × 55 cm

**Innocent Landscapes, Oristown**  2000
Colour photograph
107 × 107 cm

**Innocent Landscapes, Oristown (Twilight)**  1999
Colour photograph
107 × 107 cm

**Innocent Landscapes, Colgagh**  1999
Colour photograph
55 × 55 cm

**Innocent Landscapes, Bragan**  2000
Colour photograph
107 × 107 cm

**Innocent Landscapes, Oristown/Templetown**
2000, 1999
Colour photographs, diptych
82 × 164 cm

**Innocent Landscapes, Oristown (Night)**  1999
Colour photograph
107 × 107 cm

**Innocent Landscapes, Ballynultagh**  1999
Colour photograph
107 × 152 cm

**Innocent Landscape, Ballynultagh**  2000
Colour photograph
107 × 152 cm

**Innocent Landscapes, Ballynultagh (Twilight)**  2000
Colour photograph
107 × 107 cm

**Innocent Landscapes, Oristown (Grafti)**  2000
Colour photograph
82 × 117 cm

**Innocent Landscapes, Colgagh**  1999
Colour photograph
82 × 82 cm

**Innocent Landscapes, Ballynultagh**  2000
Colour photograph
107 × 107 cm

**Shilpa Gupta***

**Untitled**  2004–05
Interactive video projection with sound,
approx. 8 mins

**Alia Hasan-Khan**

**Kidnapped: homage to Karachi**  2004
Single channel video with sound, 3.48 mins

**Alfredo Jaar***

**Untitled (Newsweek)**  1994
17 texts and digital prints of front covers of
Newsweek magazine
54 × 38.5 cm

**Jitish Kallat**

**The Lie of the Land**  2004
6 mixed media works on handmade paper
71.1 × 106.7 cm
Courtesy of Walsh Gallery, Chicago

**Cenotaph (A Deed of Transfer)**  2007
20 lenticular prints
44.5 × 66 cm

**Amar Kanwar**

**A Season Outside**  1997
Single channel video projection with sound,
30 mins

**Dave Lewis**

**Chapter Six – Racism**  2001
33 colour photographs and text
59.4 × 42 cm

**Simon Norfolk\***

**Ascension Island: The Panopticon** 2003
Colour photograph
127 × 130 cm
The BBC World Service Atlantic Relay Station
at English Bay. Picture made 25 August to
4 September 2003.

**Ascension Island: The Panopticon** 2003
Colour photograph
127 × 130 cm
Mist-shrouded trees draped in moss along the
footpath to the summit of Green Mountain. The peak
of the mountain experiences different weather to the
rest of the island and in parts is almost tropical.

**Ascension Island: The Panopticon** 2003
Colour photograph
127 × 130 cm
The BBC World Service Atlantic Relay Station at
English Bay.

**Ascension Island: The Panopticon** 2003
Colour photograph
127 × 130 cm
Lower slopes of Sister's Peak on the edge of the
Broken Tooth Live Firing Range. The tracks have
been made by RAF 4×4s.

**Ascension Island: The Panopticon** 2003
Colour photograph
127 × 130 cm
Water catchment system built by the British military
in the 19th century in order to supply water to the
troops who manned the island. Breakneck Valley,
Green Mountain.

**Ascension Island: The Panopticon** 2003
Colour photograph
127 × 130 cm
Lava and ash formations along English Bay Road
looking towards Sister's Peak. On the edge of the
Broken Tooth Live firing Range.

**Soy una raya en el mar, Long exposure with insects:
Correr es mi destino** 2007
Colour photograph
101.6 × 127 cm

**Soy una raya en el mar, Mercury halide: Pa' una
ciuda del norte** 2007
Colour photograph
127 × 101.6 cm

**Soy una raya en el mar, Border: De la grande Babilón**
2007
Colour photograph
101.6 × 127 cm

**Soy una raya en el mar, Arizona/Sonora: Fantasma
en la ciudad** 2007
Colour photograph
101.6 × 127 cm

**Soy una raya en el mar, Desert garbage: Me dicen
el clandestino** 2007
Colour photograph
50.8 × 60.9 cm

**T.V. Santhosh**

**Another Taxi** 2004
Oil on canvas, diptych
91.4 × 243.8 cm
Collection 'The Guild', Mumbai

**Fear, Nation and False Promises** 2004
Oil on canvas, diptych
121.9 × 304.8 cm
Collection 'The Guild', Mumbai

**Peace Protest** 2003
Oil on canvas, diptych
119.4 × 303.5 cm
Collection of Minal and Dinesh Vazirani

**Gigi Scaria\***

**Raise your hands those who have touched him**
2007
Five channel video on monitors and one onto
the floor

**Fernando Traverso\***

**350, Intervención urbana, Rosario** 2001–04
23 colour photographs
30.5 × 40.6 cm

overleaf:
**Raise your hands those who have touched him**
(detail) 2007
Video still